THE HEALING POWER OF OUR PAST

THE HEALING POWER OF OUR PAST

Dr. Norton Berkowitz
Dr. Hollie Martin

iUniverse, Inc.
New York Lincoln Shanghai

The Healing Power Of Our Past

iUniverse books may be ordered through booksellers or by contacting:

iUniverse
2021 Pine Lake Road, Suite 100
Lincoln, NE 68512
www.iuniverse.com
1-800-Authors (1-800-288-4677)

ISBN-13: 978-0-595-34924-1 (pbk)
ISBN-13: 978-0-595-79639-7 (ebk)
ISBN-10: 0-595-34924-2 (pbk)
ISBN-10: 0-595-79639-7 (ebk)

Printed in the United States of America

For All Who Are Pioneers

With special thanks to our family, friends and loved ones whose patience provided us the space to persevere. To H. Robert Silverstein, M.D., F.A.C.C., and Cynthia Chase, L.C.S.W., whose professional expertise helped us plant new seeds on fertile ground. To our editor, Amanda Royce-Hale, whose guidance brought clarity to our message, allowing it to bear fruit. And most of all, thanks to all the people whose lives have touched us in ways that brought hope and healing to others.

CONTENTS

▼

Introduction

By Hollie Martin

"This book came to be because two strangers met, became friends, and unknowingly embarked on a journey together that would change both of their lives."

Norton Berkowitz, a hypnotherapist, had been practicing Past Life Regression Therapy from his home office for almost six years before we met. I had been a practicing dentist who transitioned into corporate healthcare. We lived in the same small, picturesque New England town with a quaint historic district about two blocks long centered on a patch of grass lovingly called, "The Green."

As close in proximity as we were, Norton and I were about as far apart as you could get with the structure of our lives. Norton had retired after thirty-two years of teaching in a local school district. He and his wife had successfully raised three children. All three were off on their own, exploring life for themselves and Norton and his wife began entertaining thoughts of travel and freedom, hoping to meander through their upcoming days with ease. For both, retirement was to be a welcomed reward, a reprieve from the striving of the past. They imagined it as a time for reflection and recollection of their lives' work and their relationship together. However, this path to a bucolic retirement was rudely interrupted. Norton underwent a life-changing experience that left him fascinated with hypnotherapy and Past Life Regression. As you will see in chapter one, by accident, literally, Norton's future vision was changed forever.

In distinct contrast to Norton, my life was full of hustle and bustle. The word retirement was not in my vocabulary. I was in the stage of doing, not of being, living life at full throttle. Between the demands of building a future stake in the world and raising a small daughter, my idea of relaxing was finishing the days work soon enough to have some time to plop on a couch before falling asleep in a bed. The other things I told myself I wanted to do kept moving further down a list of things I would get to eventually.

At about age 30, I switched careers. This was shocking to most of my friends and family, because the switch meant that I would abandon all of my years of training and accomplishments and enter into a future unknown. Fortunately, the change proved to be rewarding and refreshing. In my new profession, I had a chance to grow professionally and personally. I also had a chance to test my fortitude with longer hours, travel, another round of schooling, and even more demands on my time. I was testing my own limits in more ways than I could imagine.

Looking back, Norton and I now understand that our independent journeys into the new and unknown are what serendipitously allowed us to come together. We were two strangers on a similar path of discovery, and when we finally connected the purpose became clear.

These pages chronicle our journey from the days leading up to our meeting to those that followed, and the fascinating work that is the result of our collaboration. We became aware of the enjoyment others experienced when we shared the story of our relationship and the resulting changes it made on both of our lives. At the same time, we became aware that the message that we had to share could prove healing for others. This thought formed the foundation of our working relationship.

Both Norton and I were motivated by a fundamental desire to work for the benefit of others. We did not see this as some lofty ideal, but as a simple natural caring that has been with us since our individual beginnings. Norton had initially followed the path of an educator and I, that of a health worker and caregiver. We both then, unexpectedly began pursuing career options beyond our chosen professions. When we met, we were expanding our skills and experiences in ways that better served our independent inner longing for service and contribution. Although our life paths were distinctly different, our heart paths were extraordinarily similar.

What began as a client-therapist relationship soon changed, and we became friends and colleagues. We met regularly for months, recording each of our hypnotherapy sessions. In each session, Norton would ask me, while in a relaxed state, questions he had developed, with the questions in each successive session based on the information I had previously supplied. He did not tell me what he would ask ahead of time. I would then respond with clear, definite answers to all of the question asked.

Using this question and answer method, concentrating on healing applications related to regression techniques, we recorded hour after hour of responses. Soon, we realized that we were receiving information through the medium of hypnotherapy that was both useful and powerful.

Our work led to changes in the techniques Norton had previously used based on the information I supplied while in a hypnotic state. The information we received in this way changed our understanding, and as our perception changed, so too did the past life regression techniques Norton had been using. This process led to two distinct outcomes: For Norton, it allowed him to crystallize the concepts necessary to fully develop the hypnotherapeutic process for the new techniques called, *Life Memory Recall* and later, *Guided Light Therapy*. For me, the journaling of my perceptions and understandings of the information I was receiving, allowed me to translate my experiences into words. The words became paragraphs and the paragraphs became pages. Eventually, by combining my journals with Norton's client's stories of healing, this book came into being.

The Healing Power Of Our Past chronicles the development of the new therapeutic techniques and their healing potential, while also detailing the unfolding of Norton's and my work together. Additionally, it tells the fascinating stories of real people who encountered healing of various illnesses or discomforts through the use of these new techniques.

In order to accomplish this multifaceted task, Norton and I decided to write this book from Norton's perspective, as if written by a single author.

This choice allowed us to begin at the beginning. It allowed us to add the understandings we gained by working together while also taking the reader through the early part of Norton's journey as a therapist and on to the time he and I came together. By using this single voice approach, the story grows in understanding as we grew in understanding and avoids any confusion about the sequence of circumstances or who contributed what and when. Therefore, at all times, the narrative represents the combined contribution of both authors.

Reader's Note: Everything you will read is true. All names, and sometimes gender, have been changed to protect the privacy of those individuals whose stories have been told. Releases for publishing their stories are on file. It is important to note that the stories chosen for this book were chosen deliberately. We chose stories that best illustrated the extraordinary range of healing possibilities available through the use of the therapeutic techniques we are introducing, thus demonstrating the broadest scope of hope for the reader. It is important that we also note that healing results through these processes can vary widely. Results do not always come spontaneously, nor are they always dramatic or immediately evident. As with any other healing modality, one size does not fit all, and responses to these healing techniques are as individual as the people who undergo them.

CHAPTER 1

▼

NORTON'S STORY

I did not plan to become a past life therapist. Yet, here I am today. As a practicing therapist for the last twenty years, I have had time to reflect on the many twists and turns within a career that was never sought, but found me. The rewards have been beyond my imagination. One is the reward that comes from assisting others. Another is the reward of seeing a face light up with understanding and joy. I've come to realize it's what I've always done.

My desire to work with others hasn't faltered. My heart still opens and overflows when I see a new light of understanding peak in each client. I feel the joy in this as I've always felt it. The difference today is that a new understanding has brought me even greater hope for the healing of the physiological, behavioral, social, emotional, or spiritual woes that cause pain and suffering. In my evolution, I have become a conduit between those in need of healing and the healing process itself. This was not part of the plan when I started simply on a search for methods to help others. That my search would become a journey to developing a new healing technique I would never have dared to imagine. That is…until the day I died.

More than twenty years ago, I was an energetic high school teacher, enthusiastic about making a difference in young lives. I provided information and hoped that they would integrate it into their own experiences. I saw a lot of teaching around me that amounted to no more than the regurgitation of the facts, with little thought of what they meant or how to apply them. This was called learning and this learning was felt to be necessary for growth.

Fortunately for me, watching the kids for many years as they changed into young adults provided its own reward. Some even turned out pretty well. At the time, I never questioned why. I was too involved in my own life. Not only was I keeping up with a predetermined curriculum, meetings, and mounds of schoolwork, but I was also supporting my family. As a father of three, there were always things to do. The greatest difficulty was our activity level. Each child was involved in one activity or another, and it was very important to me to find the time to spend with my growing family. This is what I felt a young husband and father should be doing. This was the image I held of what a family should be. I never questioned it. Rather I pushed myself as far as I could to be a model dad, husband and financial supporter. It was important to me to measure up to what I believed was meaningful at that time.

In order to meet this self-imposed image, I continued taking on extra jobs, even though the constraints on my time tightened. The extra money these jobs brought in always seemed to be needed. Initially, even during the tight times, this was a relatively good period for my family and me. But then the warning signals appeared. The stress level had begun to take its toll on my body. During a routine visit to my physician's office, he asked, "Have you been overly stressed lately?"

"No more than usual. I'm just pretty busy and working hard."

"Well," he stated, "we've got a little problem here. Your blood pressure is quite high. I'd like to see you again in two weeks to have a second look."

"Oh, ah, sure," I stammered, giving little thought to what he had just revealed. I was, after all, a young man with a lot of responsibilities. So wasn't this pretty normal? He hadn't told me there was any concern about my heart, after all; it was only a blood pressure thing. So I brushed it off as a glitch and reluctantly set up the next visit.

A few weeks later, the doctor's less than enthusiastic tone surprised me. "Norton, I think we should discuss getting you on some medication. At your current pace, this high blood pressure could cause some problems."

"Do you really think it's necessary? I don't like taking any kind of medication, and I've had trouble with some in the past."

"We'll start on something mild and see if it does the trick."

Making light of the situation, I told my wife, took the pills, and thought that was that. This was all I needed to put the whole incident out of my mind.

One Monday morning a few weeks later I awoke feeling quite ill. It was an unusual feeling, like I was not quite in control. I could feel something was not right, yet I couldn't put my finger on it. It wasn't the familiar feeling of coming down with a cold or the flu. I felt nauseous. My entire body felt slightly off balance and dizzy, and a tiny voice was telling me that something was not right. Even so, I proceeded to get out of bed and wander downstairs hanging on to the handrail. While heading down, I was slowly overcome with the feeling that my feet were no longer on steady ground. I clung tighter to the handrail, trying not to tumble down the stairs as I headed toward the bathroom.

I was comforted when I reached the bathroom safely, yet I found myself with another dilemma. I had no idea, staring at the commode, what to do next. I didn't know whether I needed to sit on it or lean over it. I was feeling sick all over. This dilemma was quickly erased as I found I could do neither. I couldn't move an inch. A fast approaching dizziness left me breathless and utterly weak. My legs disappeared beneath me and I collapsed.

Unbeknownst to me, my small daughter had followed me downstairs. Seeing me on the floor propelled her up the stairs to awaken my wife and ask why daddy was lying on the floor in the bathroom using the toilet for a pillow? My wife, as she would later tell me, awoke with a jolt and a mission in her heart. Racing down the steps, she could see my legs jutting out from the doorway. Once by my side, she remembers the first image that came into focus. My eyes were rolled back and the whites gleamed from the reflected bathroom lights. There was absolutely no movement. My skin was beginning to take on an inhuman pallor similar to that of a drowning victim; an image my wife had recently seen. She was terrified. She recalls that all of a sudden the morning held an eerie stillness. There was nothing except the two of us frozen in a moment of sheer panic.

In an instant, the stillness was shattered by the shrill of my wife's voice. I know her as a gentle and sweet person. But that was not the person that inhabited her body in that moment. This was a woman gripped in total fear. She picked me up by the collar of my shirt and in thrusts of incredible strength she began shaking my entire body. At this point she was yelling into my unexpressive face, "How dare you die and leave me with three small children? I'm supposed to go first! Don't you dare die on me! This is not fair!" Her yelling resounded throughout the house. Our frightened children stood by, bewildered, while my wife shook the life out of me, until the miracle of her love literally shook my body back into life again.

She had acted, out of her fear and enormous compassion, as a human defibrillator. The severity of the shaking had reawakened my heart to begin beating its normal rhythm. My eyes, although still glassy, were now facing toward the front of my head. Within a few gasps, my color was returning. I was able to crawl to the couch as we waited for an ambulance.

While in the hospital, I later learned that my heart momentarily stopped due to a reaction to my medication. I was told that the pills I was taking caused an electrolyte imbalance, leading to the shutdown. It was summer and I had been doing strenuous work that had depleted my potassium level. The blood pressure medication and depleted potassium level worked together to throw off my electrolyte system. Together they created the perfect balance to cause the heart stoppage. I learned even more as I lay for a number of days in a steel-framed bed with little more to do than think about what had just happened.

The first question that popped into my head was, "How did I end up here?" All was going well. I had a little high blood pressure that was all. I was busy and working hard, that's all. And on and on this went until, finally, I resolved to take a very long and hard look at myself, an examination that demanded nothing less than pure honesty. When I finally did look deeply within myself, I began to see a picture I had not seen before.

I realized that, over time, I'd become a highly nervous individual. "Man of No Patience" could have been my name. It had crept in slowly, step by step, so I hadn't noticed it, hadn't realized how bad it had become. Looking at the I.V. bandaged to my hand, I became aware that I had bitten my nails well past their fingertips. To say I was jumpy would have been an understatement. I was beyond jumpy, more like a tightened coil waiting for release. I was tired all of the time, yet, I would find new ways to keep myself going. My nights were restless, attested to by my wife. I couldn't remember the last time I sat down to read a book for my own pleasure. In fact, I couldn't even remember the last time I sat down just to sit, rest, or reflect. The picture became clearer and clearer that I was not who I thought I was. I would have to make some changes if I didn't want to end up back in the sterile environment of an emergency room, or worse.

I was finally released from the hospital after a few days, my mind still heavy with the private thoughts that had been with me during the entire stay. I realized I needed more help than conventional medical procedures could offer. I needed to find my own means to heal myself. But, how? I knew I needed to make changes, but where was I to start?

I awoke one morning with the answer. I needed to start with me. I had to take charge of myself. If I chose to work with the doctors and medication, that would be one option. But I realized that while they would work on my body, only I could work on ME. And just maybe if I worked on me, the medication wouldn't be needed. So with the intention of eliminating the need for medication, I began to research available methods to reduce stress and lower my blood pressure. I read constantly, always seeking new information. I'm not sure how all of a sudden there was time, but enough time was made. I read about stress, anxiety and tension. I was surprised to find so much information. Having not given a care about this subject before, I wasn't aware that there were entire bookshelves devoted to this subject. My pursuit became fun, a true pleasure. Being a self-directed student provided a renewed sense of myself. In a way, I was now experiencing personally the fruits of my professional passion. I was witnessing the effects, firsthand, of my zeal for knowledge. And most importantly, I was feeling it with exuberance.

As my studies continued, I was constantly fascinated to discover new techniques and methods for reducing stress and adopting a healthier lifestyle. It was time to absorb and integrate what I was learning into my life. It was time to make some changes.

These changes didn't happen overnight. It was a slow, step-by-step process. I kept it simple. In this way, the changes began to be a part of a life that was evolving from the inside out. An image of this process, which appeared to me early on is still with me today: I discovered that learning to be healthy and unstressed was like putting together an orchestra. First, I needed to select the underscore, a base from which the rest would follow. This base was the information provided by the many books and articles I had read, as well as several classes I started to attend.

Next, I needed to select the various instruments to make up my healing symphony. The first, and easiest of these, was to start a vitamin regimen. I had found that not only would I need to address what I was putting into my body, but I would also need to address what had been missing. It felt much like the tuning of an instrument before it's actually played.

Other tunings also occurred. I changed my eating habits entirely, though slowly at first. I cut out most junk food: all the wonderful fast foods, candy, ice cream, and much of my wife's delicious baked goodies. Later I cut out things like pizza and other foods containing refined carbohydrates. It was apparent that my body had difficulty processing these foods, especially at the volume I was consuming them. It had been a pattern for me to fill up on these foods and then end my day with a walk to our local ice-cream parlor for a banana split. When I stopped this pattern of eating refined carbohydrates and other junk foods, my body began to detoxify quickly. One side effect in particular was amusing. My face broke out as though I were a teenager!

I could also sense a subtler effect throughout my body: a shift in my general energy patterns. Instead of the usual jumpy energy I was accustomed to, a calmer energy took its place. Before, I had been running on foods loaded with sugar, causing my system to fluctuate wildly. The initial energetic high lasted only briefly. When it left, I felt low and depressed. I had been acting like a kid who'd consumed a few candy bars. Now, as this jittery energy changed to calm energy, I was sleeping better, my nights weren't a restless struggle, and sleep, deep sleep, felt wonderful.

This new energy I was experiencing, while steadier than before, was more powerful. I was able to get through the demands of my day more easily. My thoughts and feelings flowed in a more consistent pattern. The nail-biting habit soon resolved itself as I changed my diet. And instead of feeling tired and exhausted at the close of each day, I felt more peaceful and unburdened. My family enjoyed this change in me and supported this process. They began changing their habits with me and found their own benefits.

Through this process I was learning some important lessons. My healing path was not only healing me, it was also healing my family. It was at this point that I realized that when we heal ourselves, we also help others. Further, I realized we don't change or heal anything outside of ourselves without first changing or healing from the inside. I was now actively doing what I had vowed to do from my hospital bed; I was changing my life, and it was altering me, and everything around me. I would not understand the impact clearly for a few more years.

*   *   *   *

The orchestra played on. A few more instruments were required before the fullness of my life score could be played out for others. The next was meditation. This practice opened in me a place of quiet and reflection. I had always been the kind of person who has a constant rush of thoughts about what had been going on and where things were going next. I'd think incessantly about yesterday's events and tomorrow's activities, never taking the time to stop and smell the roses. In fact, I thought of this particular cliché as a silly excuse used by people who were too lazy or unmotivated to push ahead. Why would anyone take the time to stop and smell a few flowers when there were so many more important things to do?

Meditation changed that. It became a marvelous way for me to clear my mind of constant worry and pressing cares, and a great source of relief and release as I let a calmness drift over me. By taking the time to sit with my own thoughts, I realized how useless many of them were. Thinking about the past was important. But holding onto any of the emotions, especially the less pleasant ones, was not. Meditation provided me with the opportunity to observe my past, let it go, and see where it brought me. I could live in the moment without a head full of old worries and what ifs. I found that a majority of my reactions were directly related to how I had dealt with things previously, and I learned to look at familiar events with a fresh eye. I was able to let go of many of the things that had caused such stress in the past, such as running a few minutes late, or not finishing a project by a self-imposed deadline.

Slowly, yet steadily, I was beginning to see that if I were to change, I would need to clear out the old habits and replace them with the new, the now. The secret was in learning to explore my past by bringing it into my current moment. Thus, I was able to gain an understanding of who I was and how I became a hospital emergency, and began to affect real change in my life. The answers were being revealed to me, even though I wasn't fully aware of their ultimately profound effect on me, and my later life's work. All I did was enjoy them, knowing that the question I had asked prior to being dismissed from the hospital was beginning to be answered.

Thus, meditation was the starting point for the deeper insights for my healing process. At first, I didn't even know it was a healing process. And I certainly didn't know that what I was experiencing would be something I could share for the benefit of others. Meditation helped me see what was important in the past and what was truly important about the future. Instead of worrying about what I had to do next, I developed patience. I questioned myself about why I was in such a hurry. I questioned why I had to have everything done NOW. Why did I have to have answers for everything that I had no control over anyway? And as my meditation practice improved and deepened, so did the quickness and validity of my own internal replies. They came forth with a calm and pleasant certainty. I saw clearly that I had been acting no differently than a cat chasing its tail; the unseen enemy I was chasing around and around was me.

What joy I felt when this picture came to mind! From my meditative silence I burst into laughter. How futile my attempts had been to control everything. How ridiculous it was for me to continue doing so. How hurtful and useless this behavior really was. So I just let it go. I sat with the feeling of emptied impatience and simply experienced what it felt like. I found myself feeling my body in a way I had never felt it before. It literally felt as though I had been a ghost and now had taken solid form. It felt incredibly good.

Later, I would understand that I had indeed been living my life as a ghost of a person. I was so busy always moving ahead of myself that I was never fully present in what I was doing or who I was with. I was moving so fast through my life that I never stopped to appreciate or pay attention to what was happening in the moment. Maybe, I thought for the first time, I should take time to smell the roses. So I did, although that particular time they were irises and daisies. Again, it felt like I was experiencing my body differently. My sense of smell was keen. My eyes roamed the surroundings, feeling the sun on my back. I found myself feeling alive, *really* alive. And I wondered why I had never stopped to do this before.

The orchestra now grew even larger, with a new section added; exercise. The first instrument was running. What began as a slow, half-mile jog turned into a daily three-mile trot. This routine added exponentially to my lowered stress and increasing energy levels. It became such an integral part of my life that I was willing to get up at five a.m. to do it. Whether it was raining, snowing or below zero, I ran. It was amazing how good it felt. And when I didn't run, it was equally amazing how much I missed it.

I took up the second instrument, yoga, to enhance my meditation with body movement. My mind was finding new energy and now my body was experiencing it in another way. The connection between the body and mind and their intricate dance was another source of curiosity. As my yoga practice progressed, I realized how blended my movement and thoughts became. Meditation and movement became one; body and mind were one.

Together, a calmer, less stressed person was emerging to the point that people started to notice. They saw the differences in me and rarely hesitated to ask why. I began to tell my de-stressing story as they began to tell me their distressing ones. Before long, I was asked to speak at numerous workshops and conferences about stress management on a personal level. Instead of taking as many odd jobs as before, I was lecturing to small groups of people. To me, I was merely relating the story of my life and the journey toward positive change. To them, I was describing a possible path for healing their own patterns of stress and anxiety. This happened at the time when stress management was becoming a popular field of study and practice.

As my lectures and workshops increased in number, so did my contacts with many wonderful people. I was often struck by the uniqueness of each individual story. Often these stories were related to patterns that kept occurring in these people's lives, patterns or cycles that seemed impossible to break. Included were overeating, smoking, and other addictive behaviors. Not only did people react negatively to their stress, but they also reacted in predictable ways. I began to expand my lectures and workshops on stress management to include this understanding. As I broadened my knowledge of the inner motivations and behaviors of these wonderful people who sought my help, they in turn expanded my consciousness. They continually stretched my understanding of the human being and its complex make-up.

Their stories introduced me to many interesting places, people and ideas. One particularly challenging idea began to fire my imagination, the possibility that there were lifetimes beyond those they were currently living, that souls were reincarnated lifetime after lifetime. Curious to learn more about this concept, I again entered a stage of self-imposed study. The works of Doctors Raymond Moody, Brian L. Weiss and Ruth Montgomery[1] provided a rich source of information. Within their body of work I found the link to the experiences presenting themselves at my workshops and lectures. In conjunction with these studies, I became aware of and fascinated with the field of hypnotherapy. I studied and learned and began to

---

1. While the authors make no endorsement, more information on the work of Raymond Moody & Brian L. Weiss, can be found on the Internet through Dr. Moody's Web site, www.lifeafterlife.com, and Dr. Brian L. Weiss's Web site, www.brainweiss.com.. Ms. Montgomery wrote several books that were published by Random House, New York, and are still available.

practice the techniques offered. Inadvertently, while using some of the relaxation techniques for stress management, I had opened the door to another turn in the road. My studies put me on a path to the unknown, and I followed it with the curiosity of a child, beaming in anticipation. Before I even realized it, I was beginning my work as a hypnotherapist. With the techniques mastered, and with great zeal, I began to offer workshops on a therapy called Past Life Regression.

At first it seemed to me as though these techniques produced great feats of imagination. The stories my clients related under hypnosis were not of this, their current lives, but of other lives full of meaning and creative vision. They "saw" themselves as characters in lives past. And it was always rewarding when these "fantasies" were shared, especially in a group setting.

The field of Past Life Regression was opening its door ever wider. I was fascinated by the revelations occurring at my workshops and pursued my work with profound interest. The more work I did, the more the stories told became real to me. It wasn't long before I began to sense connections between the past life experiences and problems in current life patterns. I became aware of the possibility that this therapy could be utilized to assist with behavior cycles these people were experiencing in the here and now. I discovered that an overeater, for example, would often have a past memory of a time of starvation or a life unfulfilled. Once these stories were recovered through Past Life Regression therapy, they could be released from the person's mind. And once this was done, it had an effect on current behavior. Whether the past life experience was believed or not, its release had the effect of relieving the current problem.

I began to take note of what was actually happening at each workshop. I began to record each session, individually or in a group format, and I studied the results of my work. I would also occasionally receive feedback at a later date. The harder I looked, the more the connections I had suspected to be true were becoming very apparent. There was indeed a connection between opening the mind to past life memories and healing an ailment in this life. I began to ask the questions, "What are we really made of? Is there much more to us that is only beginning to be discovered?" and "Can we cure ourselves of what ails us?"

These questions were actually my way of asking myself what I truly believed given the results of the work I was doing. Was my belief system open to possibilities I might have considered ludicrous before my eyes were opened by my own brush with death, an event that changed me forever?

Answers came back to me through the experiences of others time and time again. I grew to believe that this work, the work of Past Life Regression, had unexpected and powerful healing potential. I had no choice but to believe when individuals began to call or write me with their thanks for curing what had ailed them. It was no longer a matter of improving stress levels, changing eating behaviors, or the cessation of smoking; it was something much more—a deeper kind of healing was taking place. I would have to accept that there was more to this work than I could have imagined. The stories presented unlimited possibilities and, therefore, I needed to be unlimited. My beliefs needed to be unlimited. My skepticism and need for "scientific proof" required a complete overhaul. I could no longer fit my work into traditional boxes. People were getting better through this work, period. And this was what I needed to rely on as my proof. I wasn't to ask how this all worked, but rather, be willing to know that it did work. It was the only way to handle, without being constantly astounded, the amazing stories revealed and their healing effects.

As an example of the openness I was required to maintain, I'll relate a short incident that happened at one of my workshops; I gave a past life regression lecture and workshop for a large group of individuals. Now, doing this regularly, I was comfortable in this setting. Normally when I hold a workshop, we're seated in a semi-circle. After my introduction and discussion on past life regression, the participants are given an opportunity to talk. Moving around the circle, each person explains why he or she had come and whether or not each has had any previous experiences with past life regression work. Once information is satisfactorily shared, the group is readied for the work ahead. Such was the case with this particular group.

After the group had gone through the relaxation process so they would be able to experience a past life (creating an alpha state of mind similar to that used in biofeedback and transcendental meditation-conscious dreaming), a woman became notably distressed. I led the workshop as a group until I could work with this woman individually. She started to tell me the story being revealed to her. She was a young woman in the Netherlands. It was near the very end of the seventeenth century or early eighteenth century. She described her attire in meticulous detail. Next she proceeded to draw a picture of her surroundings. During her descriptions, I was aware of her increasing tension and reluctance to move forward with the information. We worked together to remove the discomfort she was experiencing as a result of what was happening. Past life regression work provides this opportunity whenever it is required. There is nothing to fear in this process. In fact, she was brought to an understanding that she could continue to relay the information in a completely relaxed and comfortable way.

Having gained her composure, she again communicated in clear detail what she was "seeing." She described a heated argument she was having with her husband. Her account revealed that his temper was a source of continual fear for this woman. The argument grew in pitch until there was rage. In his enraged state, the husband drew a gun and shot her in the chest. She died from that wound.

The session did not end here. Through the years, I've developed various techniques to assist in integrating the experience for the person. I have also developed ways of calming people so they do not feel emotionally threatened by the experience while experiencing it. She would be able to remember the information free of any misgivings at having had the experience. And to a greater degree, she would take with her the knowledge that the experience in some way was beneficial.

We continued to work together in that place somewhere between heaven and earth, that place that I didn't know existed until I started this fascinating work. All I knew at the time was that there would be a positive change, that these experiences can touch a deeper part of us that leads to healing. I brought the group back to a wakeful state, and a buzz emanated from the room. Each person was bursting to tell his or her own story. Once shared, everyone left that day filled with the excitement of exploring his or her own "imaginings."

A couple of months later, I was again giving a lecture and workshop on past life regression. To my surprise, I recognized the very striking woman who had told the story of the past husband who shot and killed her. She came over to me smiling broadly. I told her that I was glad to see her again and pleased that the incident from the previous session had not prevented her from coming back. With a glint in her eye, she said she had some very interesting things to tell me, new things that had happened to her since the last session. Her excitement and enthusiasm were contagious. She said she'd tell me when we are all sitting in the circle and sharing experiences.

When her opportunity to speak came, she began at the beginning of the situation in her past life memory in the Netherlands. She told the group how she had attended my workshop a few months previously and what had occurred. Everyone was fixed to his or her seat in anticipation of hearing this woman's experiences. Within seconds, as she proceeded, the joviality of the group shifted to astonishment. She said that prior to attending my previous workshop, she had been in a two or three-year battle with doctors to find the cause of continual chest pain. The usual diagnostic tests had revealed nothing and there had been very little help offered to alleviate her discomfort. Her fears of a heart attack or other serious ailments had been ruled out, but the chest pain persisted.

A few days after her session, she realized that her chronic pain was located in the same place in her chest where she had been shot during her past life experience. During the following days, the pain had disappeared. She related the methods I had used during her past life remembering. She recalled with incredible accuracy the process of releasing this memory. I had told her, when we had worked individually, that any memory brought to the surface could be freed from her mind, her body, her emotions, or her spirit. In the remembering, she could let go of whatever affect this had within her. And if it weren't judged as real or imagined, it would be healing to her. Whatever the images were, I assured her they would provide her with the answers she was seeking. To this, she added that she had been able to embrace what I said because she felt the honesty with which I believed this to be so.

What she said next astounded me. In her acceptance of the release that occurred, not only had the chest pain left without returning, but she also became aware of another physical healing. Her asthma also stopped troubling her. With this insight came an awareness that asthma symptoms too are located within the chest. She told the group with conviction that she was sure it was all related to her past life memory. She had done nothing else, changed nothing else. She had come to the workshop to thank me. (It is now over a dozen years since she has had the past life memory experience and her previous chest pains and asthma have not returned.)

All of my thoughts during the next few days, and probably for weeks afterward, were focused on the incident at that last regression session. What was it that she really said that created the tremendous shudder within my body after hearing her words? The answer came through me like a beacon in the dark. I was so enjoying the work I had failed to consciously recognize what this work does. *IT HEALS !!!*

"It heals" became my mantra. I repeated it over and over in my mind. The healing was only limited because my belief system had been limited. Although I knew that people were experiencing relief, I had assumed that this relief was strictly emotional or psychological in nature. I had witnessed it by seeing and hearing the after effects in people willing to explore this therapy. Every trip to the bookstore or course I had previously taken confirmed this by classifying this work under the heading of psychology. I never found it listed under physiology. Now I asked: "Could this work really affect the physical body?" The answer I heard was "yes." The "yes" had been there all the time, but my own limitations placed on this work deafened me from hearing what people had been saying for some time now. In an almost manic way, I searched my files of tapes and letters. And there it was, staring me squarely in the face. People had experienced physical changes as a result of this work.

I embarked on another quest for knowledge, literally consuming everything I could find on the subject of physiological healing through regression, although I found very little. This being the case, I then concluded that I would have to take a strong and confident stand. I would have to prove this on my own. My path once again turned without my searching for it. I proceeded with the realization that rapid physical healing effects can and do take place when the difficulties from past life memories are released. I continued without knowing how this was possible, just that it was happening. Ever since that time I've been assisting people heal physiological problems in this life by releasing problems and difficulties that have occurred in their past lives. Without questioning whether past lives are real, a true part of our make-up, I have gone out on a proverbial limb. The scientific proof would have to come later. For now, the proof would be in the outcomes of those I could help. To date, I have witnessed symptoms of arthritis, asthma, obesity, neck and back pain, migraines, and a host of other physical ills resolved through this technique.

I have discovered that healings can and do occur on multiple levels, both physical and psychological. All of us are made up of much more than the body we can see. The work of recalling past life memories has no limits. It can, and often does, challenge beliefs. And, as is the case with the people you will meet by reading their personal healing stories, their beliefs needed to change in order to heal. They *did not* have to give up their beliefs; they only needed to expand them. In fact, for those who believe in a greater power, a source or presence beyond them or some form of God, the process of expansion has been made even easier. These people already accept, in faith, that the impossible is possible. Past Life Regression therapy brings a person much closer to this place of infinite possibilities. All that is required in this work is a willingness to heal and to allow an exploration of the possibility of inner understanding.

While the method is not always easily explained, it can be compared to receiving a shot of penicillin; you do not have to believe in it for it to work. And even better, past life therapy has no negative effects. It doesn't do anything adverse to you. It only works positively. As it was with the woman who expected nothing but to satisfy her curiosity about past life regression, healing occurred without her needing to change anything. In all the years of facilitating this work, I have never witnessed a so-called negative side effect. And for many, hope is restored when all else seems to fail.

The people you will read about in the following chapters and their experiences are real. Only when requested, their names and sometimes the gender were changed. They walk and talk and go about their lives in the same way as you do. What may be different is that they all share a common thread. They have all searched for healing and in the process have been healed. Some of their stories may appear to be a fantastic journey through the imagination; yet, they are living the healing results. As for me, this is all the proof I need.

My path toward knowledge continues. I'm constantly intrigued with the latest research that science offers. As science begins to prove that our world is filled with unseen things, I take joy in knowing that one day we'll understand more than we currently do. Until then, my clients will continue to astonish me with their insights. Often, they reveal connections that can boggle the mind. It's like trying to question the size of the universe. We can imagine that it extends only so far into space and then it becomes impossible to really go further. Yet, we somehow *know* that it's out there, that it keeps going even when the mind can explore no further. How do I then know this is true? I accept the part I do know and let my mind wander and expand to encompass the rest.

It is with this thought that my path as therapist and healer has evolved. I cannot prove to anyone that we live more than one life, even many lives. I cannot prove that we can carry within our bodies memories of previous events. What I do know is that we are always a part of our past. In my case, my eating habits, which had added to the ill health I experienced and the resulting high blood pressure, stemmed from lessons taught to me in my youth. Like many of you, my parents continually told me to finish everything on my plate. While this lesson was meant to instill gratefulness for what I had by recognizing that there is a world of have-nots, it only produced a sense of guilt. At one time, I was literally afraid to leave behind any uneaten food that had been placed before me. Not until I saw the irrational connection between what I was taught and what was happening in my reality, was I able to change.

In dealing with phobias in my work with others I have found similar connections. A fearful incident in childhood would be carried into one's adult life. The incident, long forgotten by conscious memory, could still be present. Through hypnosis, the incident could be recalled. Once the person releases this fear from the child's perspective, the phobia is released. For example, childhood experiences of playing with matches or falling down a flight of steps might reveal themselves in the adult as fear of fire and high places. Again, my experience has shown me that once the memories are recovered, the person can be healed. Life Memory Recall, a modified technique of Past Life Regression therapy I have developed, works in this way. A memory exists and is evoked in order to bring into this life a meaning that results in healing. The childhood experience exists, and even though it may be completely out of rational context, it is real to the person who is experiencing it. Because it is real, it can be released.

In my own healing path, I've come to accept this as fact. And like the universe example, I can only go so far. I can't answer why my parents told me what they did. They simply did. And their parents did, and so on. The result is the same. A belief was created in the past that affected the present. And by working through the past, remembering an incident long ago and releasing it with a new understanding, I've been able to make the changes necessary for my own healing.

When we recover our past lives, incidents may be revealed that have meaning in the present. When these incidents are released, we heal. Just as the example of cleaning my plate was passed on for generations in my family, so too, may be the experiences of other lives. It's easy to see the effects of the experiences in our current life from our childhood; it's much harder to imagine what the effects are if events or memories are centuries old. If these are the images our mind holds onto, whether lived or perceived, then they need to be brought to the surface. Life Memory Recall therapy allows this to happen so that change may occur. And I see people heal everyday as a result.

My hospital bed question of how I ended up as a near statistic has been sufficiently answered since that dreadful morning long ago. Physically and mentally I've changed. I've healed. Emotionally and spiritually I continue to change. My lectures, workshops, and private sessions with individual clients never cease to amaze me. The experiences people have force me to look deeper into the place of all possibilities. I can no longer say what's real and what isn't. The minute I think I've heard a phenomenal and impossible story, it is matched with yet another.

At first, regardless of content, my natural skepticism placed the experiences in the realm of fantasy. I was reluctant to believe any of it was real, just as you readers may be reluctant to view past lives as real. Yet, after listening to many taped conversations of my clients, a pattern emerged. There were consistencies within their stories that I couldn't ignore. Was it possible for a human being to experience something beyond our wildest dreams? Could useful information be retrieved from a source unknown? It wasn't until I studied the evidence long and hard that it yielded a picture of a human being revealed on many levels. No longer could I separate the body from the mind, the mind from the emotion, or the emotion from the spirit. All of these levels of being were necessary and infinitely intertwined. And only when viewed as a connected whole, did I finally see what work was ahead of me.

With this came the beginnings of an understanding of the purpose of my work. I was to continue working as a therapist. I was to acknowledge that Life Memory Recall is a healing therapy, and I was to bring this to anyone who asked for help in his or her own search for healing. I could offer hope either on an individual basis or to many people in the form of lectures and workshops. The sharing of the information and the findings of the work needed to expand in even greater ways. This last direction has shown me who I am, how I got to where I am, and where I might be going. It has affected me at all the levels of my being, and brought my own healing process to a point of near completion.

It was at this point in my life that a new client appeared at my door one day in late summer. I was expecting a routine session and exploration into a past life memory. She was curious, like most of the people I work with. After we had spoken for a short time, I realized we had something in common. She, like me, had a near death experience, although hers occurred when she was less than two years old. This peaked my desire to work with her. Together, we went through the techniques for inducing the state of relaxation hypnosis affords. The session went along as I expected as she remembered the incident of her near death. She was comfortable and very communicative. She re-experienced the event with ease.

Normally, at the moment of "seeing" the separation from this life to the next, the release of this experience follows and the "seeing" ends. Only, this time it did not. She continued past the experience and traveled to a place she described as unfamiliar. I asked for descriptions. She responded with clarity. I thought we were nearly finished, and was about to bring her back from the hypnotic state, when she decided differently. She said we were not finished and that she needed to return back to the place she had described earlier as "joy". There was someone there who wished to speak to us.

Not knowing where this was going, but feeling inside that something important was happening, I proceeded. I was no longer asking the questions as I normally would, she was asking them of me. Then she began telling me things about myself, answering the inner questions I had with regard to the past life work I was doing. And in clear responses, she addressed my skepticism. She brought together the pieces in my *maybe* drawer. I had never had any doubts about bringing my work to others, but as she spoke, the intensity of my resolve turned into a more compelling drive. Her tone never wavered. It remained soft and gentle, yet firm in its delivery. As she proceeded, the separation between my work and myself faded. There was no separation. The picture was clear and complete. I was as much a person being healed as a healer.

The process of healing works both ways beautifully. We are all in this together. It was time to share what I knew, and as I share it with others they will do the same. And the healing process will be expanded so it becomes available to *everyone*. For the first time, I really saw *me*. I realized that I had always wanted to help people; that I always wanted to offer what I could. My path had always been clear, but I chose not to see. With eyes now open, I was left filled with gratitude from this experience. It touched me at new levels of my being. I saw then why I had to end up in the hospital. It was the only way to get my attention! As a result, my life path changed instantly. It was a gift in disguise; a gift that I could now share by writing the experiences of the many lives that have been healed by a method that found its way to me. Just as they've touched me, I offer their stories to you. Just as these people have been healed, Life Memory Recall may help to heal you.

I continue my work daily. The learning never stops, it only deepens. My path has been set. And as far as the woman who opened my eyes enough to stand up in my beliefs, I now call her my friend. Her extraordinary story is told here. And our story together has taken the form of this book.

CHAPTER 2

▼

THE SAMURAI

Carlos was twenty-two when he came to see me. I recognized him from a workshop I had held about a year before on Past Life Recall. He did not particularly stand out in the group, yet, I remembered his intensity, because it was unusual in such a young man. He had a weightiness, a sense of contained control about his posture. When I spoke, he really listened and looked at me directly. It was obvious that he was not a boy finding himself, but a man who knew where he stood. He exhibited an air of confidence that belied his years. It had been a pleasure working with him in the group and seeing his willingness to follow my lead. Even so, he had revealed nothing about Carlos, the person. So while I remembered him, I did not feel that I knew him. I welcomed the opportunity to learn more.

Once settled in, Carlos began to describe his experience at the workshop. He told me it had opened his mind to the benefits of Past Life Recall. He said he had been able to "see" a past life and had found it exciting. He also said he left the workshop with a wonderful feeling that lasted for a number of days. It was more than just being relaxed. It was a total sense of well-being.

But he went on to say that what brought him to me for individual work was a different matter. After those first few days following the workshop

Carlos's life proceeded as before. The same stresses reappeared and things went on in the usual way. He said he was happy enough, but that he was dealing with some problems that he had developed early in his life. One of them was a persistent and often painful stomach ailment that had plagued him since childhood. It was characterized by periods of intense pain and chronic indigestion and diarrhea, and it had never been cured completely despite his family's best efforts. At times, the pain was so severe that he often missed school.

By the time he was sixteen, he was taking a prescription antacid daily because he had been diagnosed with ulcers. Initially the medication provided temporary relief, but the problem never went away. After several months he and his family realized it was not helping much and he discontinued its use. The stomach flare-ups persisted whether he took the medication or not.

Other attempts had been made to find a cure. Some of the treatments helped for a while, but then the symptoms would return and the search for help would begin all over again. While it was fortunate that the episodes of severe pain were short-lived, the ever-present indigestion and diarrhea began to erode Carlos's quality of life. Not understanding the cause, he was completely at a loss when it came to understanding how to care for his condition. As hard as he tried, he was unable to connect his actions with the end results.

He found that if he did not eat, the symptoms stayed away long enough so that he could go about his business. He was temporarily able to perform his job and maintain his daily activity level. However, while this approach allowed him to function in a relatively normal way without excess pain hindering him, continuing for any length of time on an empty stomach was extremely draining. So finally he would eat, feel reinvigorated for a short time, and then the pain would return, creating a vicious cycle.

In an attempt to try to break this cycle, Carlos tried a number of prescribed diets. Some of these diets worked temporarily, at least for short periods of time. But his level of frustration grew when he found that the very same foods that had not bothered him the day before might induce cramping and indigestion the next day.

Over time there were other medication choices to consider; new and improved drugs were continually coming to market. Inevitably, when he tried one or another, it would work for a while, but then his condition would revert to its previous state. For Carlos, the results were predictable and exasperating. Somehow, though, he learned to live with his condition well enough to accomplish his goals and move on with his life.

But now, Carlos's patience and acceptance were wearing thin. Recent bouts of severe pain had left him anxious and tense. The memory of the feeling of well-being he experienced after the past life recall workshop led Carlos back to me. He was ready to explore new avenues for his health, and he was convinced that the methods I used in my past life regression work could help him relax, and perhaps even lessen the frequency and severity of his episodes of pain. He also remembered my words about healing in my lecture prior to the hypnosis workshop. He recalled my stating that by bringing past life memories to the present and using a method for releasing them, a person's present state could be altered positively. He even quoted me saying, "If that state is one of ill health, the reward can be wellness." I had cited a few examples of this for the group participants and assured them of their validity. Physical changes can and do occur by using this form of healing therapy. Carlos had heard every word and remembered my lecture well. He was ready to start the process and try it for himself.

I began by guiding Carlos into a comfortable, relaxed state and helped him journey in his mind to a tranquil, conflict-free place away from the stresses of every day.[1] I regressed Carlos, guiding him to a virtual paradise, a white sand beach in midsummer. I had suggested the beginning scene, as I routinely do for most of my clients, to help Carlos with the visualization

---

1. The first part of the Past Life Recall process assists a person in reaching this place and its peaceful state of being; a vacation for the mind. Just as an ocean swim or an isolated ski trail can at the same time relax and invigorate our outer bodies, finding this spot does wonders for our inner awareness. From this place our minds can do what they do best—create. They can experience open adventures, without normal limits and constraints, while producing images that feel wonderful, real, and pleasing to the inner senses.

process. He found this paradise quickly. From there, my verbal guidance took the form of suggestions to help his mind to relax even further and draw a picture for itself. I suggested the sandy beach only as a starting point and then helped him to paint his own images. As he filled in the detail, his visions began to become clear and rich. It is at this point in the session that the mind is relaxed enough to explore its greater depths. As Carlos related what he saw he became the tour guide for me. I became as much the follower as the facilitator, matching him turn for turn and occasionally steering around a few obstacles.

As I guided Carlos ever deeper into the experience, he was soon following along easily with my gentle directions. With the visualization process firmly established and Carlos responsive, I asked Carlos to look for a stream somewhere in his paradise. He found it without much of a pause. I asked him to "see" a bridge stretching across it. This he also readily found and began to relate the detail of his vision. He was beginning to create for himself his own images, images that would lead him to a place where he could be healed by what his mind would reveal.

The bridge I had asked him to find was, according to Carlos, arched and made of bamboo. He approached the bridge, ready to move forward. Before he started to cross it, I told him he could go ahead whenever he was ready. He could take his time or run. He could look around when he was on it. He could do whatever he wanted before he reached the opposite side. And when he reached the other side, I told him he would be in another life, a past life that he could see. It would be a life that would help him to discover the source of his stomach problems. The answer would be there. With those assurances, I suggested that he was ready to cross. Carlos took it from there.

He told me he was in feudal Japan in 1562. The date slipped off Carlos's lips without any hesitation, as did his descriptions as he journeyed forward from the first step over the bridge. I asked him if he knew who he was. He was initially uncertain. I suggested he look at his hands. Was he male or female, young or old? Could he clearly see how he was dressed? Could he tell me more about this person in Japan? After a short pause, he began to speak clearly.

He was a male in his mid-twenties. His name was *Usoki*.

I continued the questioning, "Who is *Usoki*?"

"He is a Samurai."

"Would you describe what he is wearing? Can you see what he is wearing?"

"I have a pleated skirt-like pants on called an *ahcomma*. They are black. My shirt is white, a *gee*."[2]

"What is a gee, Carlos?" I asked, needing to become as familiar with the person as Carlos seemed to be. Although my knowledge of early Japanese culture was limited, it soon became apparent that Carlos' was not.

"It's the top that we use when we train. Socks and sandals".

"Do you have anything on your head?"

"No, I just have my hair pulled back"

"Hair pulled back into what? How is it pulled back?"

"A little (brief pause) ponytail."

"And what are you doing?"

"*Usoki*," he responded.

"What are you doing now, *Usoki*?"

"I am walking."

"Are you carrying anything with you while you're walking? Do you have any weapons?"

---

2. It is important for me to note, that the spellings used are of my making based on the way they sounded to me at the time of the session. Occasionally, I will ask for spellings. In this case, because there were quite a few words used, I decided it would disrupt the flow of the past life memory experience. I also realized that even if I asked for a spelling, I wouldn't know if I was getting a translated spelling or an actual spelling. Japanese words may not translate directly, instead may represent a phrase or a meaning quite different than its English counterpart. Therefore, for this session, the spelling of unfamiliar words are based on the phonetic expression provided in the taped conversations. With some research on my part, many words have proven legitimate and their spelling corrected. In Carlo's case, some words have been found while others remain unknown. For this reason, unfamiliar words are italicized. Detail beyond this is actually unimportant since the healing that happened, occurred, regardless of whether the words of another language are confirmed as existing.

"Yes. I have my two swords by my side."

"Two swords. Tell me about those two swords." I persisted. My interest was growing. Not only would I continue to guide Carlos through his memory, but he would also guide me into an unknown world. I would become his student as much as I was his teacher, and I was fascinated.

"My main weapon is the *gatana* or *katana*. It is the longer one of these two. I wear it any time I am outside of my home."

"Um, hmm," I muttered while taking notes.

"And my smaller weapon is called the *wakashaki*, it is about half the size and I keep that one on me ALL the time, even when I'm sleeping," Carlos said with seeming pride at his sense of ownership.

"Why do you have two weapons?"

"It's part of my training—should I lose one, I have the other."

"And how long have you been training?"

"Since I was a child."

"About how old?"

"Hard physical training since about six years old. But it's been a part of me since I was born."

"How come, since you were born?" I asked, confused by this response.

"It's in my family. My father was one too, a Samurai like me."

My head filled with many questions regarding his early life. I would have enjoyed exploring this aspect of Carlo's past life memory further, wondering what it was like for a little boy whose life was predetermined. I wondered what his family was like and how he interacted with the other family members. But, as a past life therapist for many years, I knew my role was to keep moving forward so Carlos could find the answers he was looking for. Slowly, but enthusiastically, I continued on, guiding Carlos through this memory toward the goal of finding the point of this past life that would heal the problem he had in the present.

"Do you like being a Samurai?"

"Yes."

"Why?"

"I love the fighting," he said without a hint of emotion.

"Um hmm. Are you afraid of being hurt or injured?"

"No."

"Why not?" I inquired. Working with many on releasing phobias and fears, I always jumped at the chance to get a closer look at why they existed and how to release them. In Carlos's case, I was presented with the opposite situation, because here was someone telling me he had none.

"I'm good," he said. It was that simple. While it was not quite the response I was hoping for, nonetheless, it was perfect for him. Carlos continued, "It's part of my training—to not fear death."

"Do you speak Japanese? Can Carlos speak Japanese? Did Carlos know Japanese before?"

"Only a few words."

"Well, I'd like you to speak not as Carlos but as *Usoki*, okay? Talk to me in Japanese." [3] He responded in what sounded like Japanese without any perceived effort.

"Can you say anything else?"

"It's strange, it doesn't seem like it makes sense," he said.

"Say it anyway," I responded.[4] I assured Carlos that it didn't matter what he was saying, that he only needed to repeat what he was hearing.

Accepting this, he continued. The answer sounded like gibberish to me, yet I knew it could be important to Carlos later.

---

3. The purpose of my question was to benefit Carlos. Each person I work with receives a taped copy of the conversations we have. Often, during the session, information is revealed that is foreign to the individual, but, the information becomes credible when he or she researches it. It may be information about a particular place, a family lineage whose names can be discovered, or events that are known only to those in scholarly pursuit on a given topic. For Carlos, it would be knowledge of a language not part of his current life experiences.

4. In hypnotic states our own sense of self is not lost. The subject remains aware of self at all times. Nothing can be suggested that would interfere with a conscious reaction. For Carlos, he would indeed think he was speaking gibberish in his fully wakeful state. He was hearing the sounds clearly, yet in his awareness they did not make sense. When received images are unclear to the conscious personality of the self, one tries to assess them. This is what Carlos was trying to do. All he needed was my permission as his guide to allow *Usoki* to speak freely.

"Uhmm, what else?"

Again, I could not interpret Carlos's response, but I persisted. "Tell me something about yourself in Japanese; about your life," I stated. And again he responded with more sounds, different each time.

"Okay. What did you say? In English, please."

"I am a Samurai."

"Okay," I said and moved on. Carlos could do the research later. "Do you fight in many battles? In many wars?"

"Yes."

"Why do you fight? What do you do when you fight?"

"I fight because it's my duty."

"Duty to do what?" I persisted.

"To serve my lord. It's part of the Samurai. I am honor-bound to serve."

"Now, do Samurai go from one lord to another, or not? And what is the name of your lord?"

Pause. "*Hakimi*."

"*Hakim*i?"

"Yes. He's big. He likes to live life."

"And what do you do to defend him?"

"Whatever he wants me to."

"What would that be? Tell me some of the things you would do," I stated, hoping he would elaborate. As he was speaking, I could already see and hear a change taking place in his personality. His voice became clear. He was definite in his responses. His tone was self-assured and his posture straightened as he sat on my couch. The change in his persona suggested that rather than seeing himself as a Samurai, he had become the Samurai. And he was obviously pleased to be telling me his story.

"I may have to do something as simple as taste his food. To check for poison or maybe having to fight for him."

"Who would you fight? Another lord or what?"

"It could be some peasants who are not happy, or it could be a *Ronin*, a wandering Samurai trying to make money, or a Ninja.

"And there are *Ronin* Samurai?"

"Yes, they are wandering Samurai. They have no masters. They tend to work by themselves."

"As individuals? What do they do?"

"Some of them just test their skills, getting better. Others, they take jobs for money. Sometimes they kill people."

"Um, hmm. Now how many Samurai does your lord have?"

"Maybe about seventy. My lord is *Resagee*. His palace is in Osaka. Our main job is to fight, to defend the castle for the lord. We protect the palace from peasant uprisings, from other lords wanting my lord's lands. Some are food testers all the time. Some are messengers. Some are kind of like liaisons for the town."

"And you do a lot of different jobs?"

"Yes."

"Uh, huh. What job do you like the most?"

"I love the fighting."

"You love to fight?" I continued without waiting for a response, "You mentioned the Ninjas; what about the Ninjas?"

"They're assassins."

"They're assassins? Are they very good at what they do?"

"Not good enough."

"Why do you say that?"

"None of them have beaten me yet." Carlos's voice reflected a clear sense of pride.

"Um, hmm. And have they tried?"

"Yes. They tried to get in, usually at nighttime. Someone is able to sound an alarm, or sometimes I have been able to spot them myself. All it takes is one little mistake."

"Like what?"

"Walking too loudly."

"And the Samurai walk the areas all the time?"

"Yes. There is always someone patrolling around the castle. Ninja, they are just low, they're scum. Samurai...we have much honor. We never strike a man when he is running. You don't hide. We fight out in the open. Ninjas use whatever they can to win. They have no honor. When I am able to fight them, face-to-face, and defeat them, it is one of the greatest honors and pleasures."

"Do Samurai normally win against a Ninja?"

"I do."

"Some don't, huh? How do you even contact a Ninja? How do you find one?" I pressed since Carlos's responsiveness increased with each of my questions.

"You don't go to Ninjas, they go to you. Whenever they come into the castle, it hasn't been often that they come up to the castle. Usually I spot them, or something gives them away. They are in families."

"They're in families. And you go to the families if you want them to assassinate someone, is that it?" I asked. My curiosity increased as enthusiasm and growing details also increased.

"You don't usually know who their families are. They are good at disguising themselves."

"Do you have a family?" Now, I could return to a point that focused more specifically on *Usoki*.

"I did."

"You did? Married? Any children?"

"No."

"What happened? You say you did have a family?"

"Well, I had parents. I never married."

"Oh I see. Do Samurai marry?"

"Sometimes, not often."

Carlos's responses became shortened when he answered questions that seemed to have little concern for him. Because I still had not arrived at a place where anything in this past life memory seemed to apply to Carlos' daily physical struggles, I decided it would be best to continue with my questions about his life as a Samurai. The many turns that most Past Life Recall sessions take are often necessary to get a clear picture in order to find a related cause for the present life's situations. Carlos's session was no exception. The information leading to Carlos's healing would be revealed, but it would happen in Carlos's time, not mine. My task was to keep asking the questions until the right one was unveiled. All questions, however, are important to help arrive at the sought-after healing. So changing my line of questioning, I returned to, "What would you like to tell me about the Samurai?"

"They were masters at what they did."

"Do they have guns?"

"We don't use guns"

"No? Why?"

"It is not honorable to shoot. We fight face-to-face, hand-to-hand. The Ninja learned how to use guns."

"The Ninja learned to use guns, but Samurai don't?"

"No. There is no honor in guns. Sometimes we would have foot soldiers that would use guns, but those are mostly the big, big battles."

"Tell me more about being a Samurai. Anything you want to tell me; the way you live, the way you exercise, the way you learn to do your things, your weapons, or anything you wish to tell me, that you find interesting."

Carlos had become comfortable with our interaction to the point of returning the information seconds after the last word I spoke. We were again on track to a path Carlos obviously wanted to take. His desire to speak about his life as a warrior, filled his voice with a genuine lilt while still maintaining its air of prideful boasting.

"I usually wake up before dawn, before the sun even comes up, to start my meditation. I meditate for maybe an hour, and as the sun comes up I finish my meditation. Then I wash myself with a cold bath so I can be invigorated, and then I practice. Generally the first thing I practice is with my sword. I practice alone. Later in the day we usually get together and practice in our *dojo*. Our meals are kept simple and are only eaten after the morning's practice. We eat rice, tea, pickles and vegetables. We eat just what we need to sustain ourselves. Then we practice again."

"I want you to go through your practices so Carlos will understand how beautiful and how easy it is. Then Carlos can automatically take that into himself, be a Master also."[5]

As was discussed in Chapter one, we are at any given moment the result of our past moments. In Carlos' situation, it seems that he was living a

1990's version of his former life as a Samurai, at least certain aspects of it. As obvious as this connection was, Carlos still had not found the aspect of his past life memory that could help him find the cure he was looking for. I was certain, however, that it would be found. I knew the place to begin was to empower Carlos with *Usoki's* self-confidence.

"Let's start with the sword and go through the practice," I began, "so Carlos can learn the practices and FEEL the sense of what it's like. Feel the gracefulness of it. Go through it all so Carlos will learn, feel, and know the good that will come from it. When you're through with this and Carlos feels it, let me know."

There was no immediate response, so after waiting a substantial amount of time, I rephrased my suggestion as a question. "Good practice?"

"Yes!" he exclaimed emphatically.

I continued, "Now, you're at the *dojo* and you're practicing and you're REALLY feeling good because you are at your best. Go through the practices so Carlos can be as fluid, as good as *Usoki*. Let Carlos know and understand it so when he is working out, it won't be him, it will be you, the Samurai working out. He will feel the same wonderful sense that the Samurai had, with the extraordinary ease that *Usoki* had. Go through it."

"It is poetry in motion," he said after a long pause.

"Poetry in motion? Did you do well?"

"Yes!"

"Are there very special moves that you, *Usoki*, do that Carlos doesn't know about? Show Carlos so he will know what they're like, because he has never seen these, has he?"

---

5. In the many years of doing Past Life Recall work, it has been more common than not to find connections between the exposed memories and the motivations for current life activities. During our discussion prior to beginning the hypnosis and Past Life Recall, Carlos had briefly mentioned that in his current life he was working as a Tae Kwon Do instructor. This livelihood taught him the discipline of mind over matter, which helped him overcome his physical obstacles. Although they were still present, it gave him the fortitude to continue his life as normally as possible. He had been drawn to this work, which he described as finding a passion. It satisfied him in many ways.

"No."

"Show Carlos now."

Again he paused for a considerable length of time.

"Does Carlos understand these now?"

"Yes."

"And Carlos could do these now?"

"Yes."

"Is there anything else that you should show Carlos so he could become even better and move up to third, fourth, or fifth black belt, very quickly and easily?"

The next response was surprising. "Nothing that I could show him, but something that he needs to understand."

"And what is that?"

"He has to develop the spirit too."

"And how do you do that?" I queried.

"Understand that a Samurai can die at any moment. Enjoy everything around you. Enjoy life. Enjoy animals. Enjoy the women. Enjoy the plants. Cultivate your spirit. Don't just focus on the physical."

"Can you convey that to Carlos?"

"Yes."

I pursued, "It is as much spiritual as it is physical, is that what you are saying?"

"Yes."

"And the spirit must come in. Where does the spirit come in to?"

"It comes into you, it comes into everything."

"Is it held in any place special? Where?"

"Just below the navel. The center of our energy, where our *ki* comes from."

"Does Carlos know that?"

"Yes. He knows it; he just doesn't understand it. He isn't quite with it."

Aware of the importance of the information given by *Usoki* and its importance for Carlos's life, I guided him gently into accepting what was being said. "Carlos, permit it to come in so you feel it, and sense it, and know it. And tell me when you feel that, Carlos."

Following yet another pause, I questioned, "It's a powerful sense. It is, isn't it? Are you accepting it now?"

"Yes."

"It fills you with energy."

"Um, hmm." Carlos's face softened with this barely audible answer.

"It's an energy you keep within and you get so much of it that you can release it to other people, right?"

"Yes."

"It just flows right through you."

"It IS connected to everything," he said as if he suddenly realized what had happened to him.

"Take your time and tell me when you are done bringing in this energy now." I received an "okay" moments later.

We proceeded with more questions and answers until we arrived at the part of *Usoki's* life that would have an impact on Carlos's life today. As before, details of the Samurai life continued. *Usoki* moved with grace through the expression of his prowess and pride as a warrior and related aspects of his life until he related to me a time of defeat, both in battle and in personal spirit.

Usoki's Lord *Resagee* died in battle at age seventy. He had been ambushed and stabbed in the back. It was the Samurais' duty to protect him and they failed. A rival clan took over and their Lord *Jeray* became the new ruler. Because a Samurai was sworn to serve a single lord for life, duty to a new lord was unthinkable. In disgrace for losing the battle and the life of Lord *Resagee*, there remained one last thing for *Usoki* to do. He would commit seppuku (the equivalent of Hara Kiri), the ritual suicide of the Samurai warrior to end his service in honor. The procedure was to plunge his *katana*, his long sword, into his stomach and cut a 'Z' into his abdomen. Death was assured by the disembowelment, beheading followed. This is what *Usoki* did and his life ended at age thirty.

As horrible as this scene may sound, especially since Carlos was re-experiencing this event, Carlos remained calm and comfortable during the session. If Carlos had become uncomfortable, as a facilitator of this process, I would have been able to redirect the feelings while still allowing the past life memory to unfold.[6]

Carlos was not only calm after the session, but elated! Yes, even after witnessing his (*Usoki's*) own death, Carlos felt happy. I questioned the smile on his face. He told me that as the past life memory reached its end, something felt released from him. He described it as a kind of tension that went away. I told him that this response was very common and that he should pay attention to what happens after the session. He left my office with one last suggestion from me, "Just relax and enjoy the feeling, the meaning of your past life memory will present itself in its own time and own way. The good news is that when it does, you'll know what it means for you."

The following day, Carlos experienced the healing he desired. Pain, diarrhea, and indigestion were gone. Vanished! It has remained so to this day, not a symptom having returned.

Carlos' past life memory had ended with the release of the Samurai's death experience. Through this therapy, he was able to reintegrate this past experience into his current life. He gained the simple recognition that *Usoki's* life was a part of Carlos's inner knowing. The memory of the Hara-Kiri was somewhere and somehow retained within Carlos's mind. Its place needed to be recognized as a past event. Whatever Carlos held onto from this past life memory was returned to its rightful place, the past. While Carlos realized that the event was *Usoki's* and not his own, he also understood that it was but a leftover fragment within the recesses of his own mind. How it got there, we do not know for sure. What is important is what happened when it was returned to its owner.

---

6. I have learned to let the experience go forward as needed without interfering unless a certain level of discomfort becomes evident. For my clients, they are often less reactive to the experience than I am. I have learned that the process is a refined dance between my client, the information and me. Together, based on practice, the experience is allowed to be what it needs to be while getting to where it's going in a comfortable way.

A few weeks after our session, Carlos contacted me with audible excitement in his voice. After exchanging our hellos, he expressed his joy at the "side effects" he was experiencing as a result of our previous session.

"Side effects? What side effects?" I asked.

Carlos quickly told me about his last encounter with his martial arts instructor. While practicing his form, Carlos noticed that his moves were absolutely fluid, and they appeared to be performed spontaneously without previous thought. Carlos had discovered that he could perform new moves and holds he had not known before he had experienced *Usoki* in my office. He had remembered them effortlessly from the morning Samurai practice *Usoki* had shown him while going through the past life memory. The look on his instructor's face was reason enough to call me, he said. We shared a few more words and then went happily on our way.

The healing effect Carlos experienced may seem miraculous, and it certainly was astounding, but it is not an isolated case. I will share with you several more healing experiences in this book that will show you that this type of healing is the rule rather than the exception. I will also be sharing stories of healing that go beyond this type of healing, healing that will occur in ways never expected.

CHAPTER 3

▼

IS THIS FOR REAL?

Are you wondering if the story you just read is real? I can tell you that it is the true story of a real person who had the results they needed in their life. The healing of a long-standing physical problem occurred and has been sustained for a number of years. Carlos even had fun with his experience by bringing in another piece of his past life remembrance, which he used for his own enjoyment. Yet, does this mean that Carlos' experience was "real" in the way we normally define the term? No.

The common definition of reality is insufficient to answer this often-asked question accurately. A new understanding of how we define what is real is required. It must take into account that people, more times than not, when confronted with past life memories, wonder whether they are actual events or flights of imaginary make-believe. They presume that only actual events or the memory of actual events determine the nature of what is real, and relegate anything not provable as such to the realm of fantasy. This renders anything gleaned from the imagination alone as inconsequential. This is a normal response when the definition of reality is narrow. It is neither good nor bad. It is just a fact that I work with everyday.

To many, past life memories are assumed to be no more than a recollection of a story once read or a combination of previously known facts creatively pulled together. It is understandable that this should occur when someone is assessing this work without the benefit of an expanded definition of "real". However, I have witnessed on many occasions how this viewpoint completely changes when someone experiences the Life Memory Recall process. It changes because the information retrieved affects their present lives. The affects are seen and felt as an outcome of the experience. The result, in essence, is what makes the experience real. The fact that the experiences themselves, regardless of their source, have a positive impact in people's lives is what "real-ly" matters.

The dictionary tells us that "real" is defined as something occurring or existing as fact. Authenticity is that which is in agreement with fact. Under these definitions, it is a fact that information is retrieved during a past life memory session. The experience of remembering or rediscovering information then becomes an authentic experience. And what does this mean? It means that we can use words we have to describe an experience that's hard to explain. Combined, the words "real" and "authentic" portray a meaning consistent with the ordinary understanding and definitions associated with them. But do these words give a complete picture of past life memory experiences and validate the healing effects of these experiences? The questions become, "Where's the proof?" and "Will changing the way I define these experiences change the outcome?"

To begin to answer these questions, a greater understanding of the process is needed. All past life memory stories, the process of remembering them, and the results achieved are based on individual experience. Each story and its related outcomes are as unique as the clients I help. The reality of the stories people tell cannot be measured by a consensus based on a single, preconceived and accepted definition. By moving beyond the accepted definition of reality, the individual becomes free to define what is real to them. Thus, they may allow the Life Memory Recall experience to be whatever they want or need it to be. It is as real as the individual chooses to make it. The good news is that I have seen it become something helpful, even when someone makes it out to be nothing much more than make-believe. Later, many change their minds.

For those who have experienced a healing through this therapy, choosing to believe that the experience was an authentic event became important only after the healing event took place. It did not matter what they felt about this work prior to their experiences. They could accept or reject the therapy as they wished. The answer to the question of proof or the "realness" of their experience was allowed to flow comfortably and without suggestion. Proof of "realness" was accepted when an individual experienced an undeniable healing. The reality of an individual's improved well-being validates the reality of the experience because of that healing. And this is all the proof most people want or need.

How a person defines the experience during or after the therapy doesn't appear to interfere with the results a person receives. However, what a person thinks about these experiences before the experience occurs does seem to make a difference on what becomes of the experience. For example, when a person accepts the concept that the definition of what is real can be expanded, it may also lead to an acceptance of the possibility that another source of healing exists. We are then presented with tantalizing evidence of a source of healing that is effective when other efforts have failed or when the results have been less than desirable. This you will see in chapters to come in the stories of people who have been helped by Life Memory Recall.

I have been privileged to conduct many group workshops across the country. Generally in these workshops a light and jovial atmosphere prevails. Most individuals are drawn there out of curiosity or by referral. The results obtained from a group setting are different from those experienced through one-on-one or private sessions. In a group setting, the participants' regression to a past life may not be as detailed or are sometimes constrained by time limitations. However, usually all in attendance experience something of a past memory, and occasionally a particular individual in the group will become deeply immersed in their past experience which may then be shared by all. The sharing is done by allowing group members who are no longer participating in retrieving memories to write down questions. I will then talk to the person I am individually regressing (a hypnotherapeutic term for moving backward through time while in a relaxed state) and they are free to respond to me.[1] The group-to-individual arrangement is always agreed upon by all group participants at the start of the session. It inevitably leads to a lively and interactive discussion following the more detailed, individual regression experience.

Just this type of situation occurred for a young woman who attended one of my large workshops. Her life memory experience began when she identified herself as a woman living someplace in the South of what was colonial America. Drawing her out, I asked her if she could tell us what was happening. She stated clearly that she and many others were celebrating in the streets. When asked why, she responded, "We had evidently written some type of letter. A proclamation to England that said we were breaking off ties with them."

"Do you know, can you see what year it is?"

"1776."

"Do you know the month?"

"July."

Of course, I silently thought and proceeded to ask her the day. We all felt we knew without expressing it that she was about to say the 4th. To our amazement she did not! Her response was, "July 2nd."

I asked again and received the same answer. I found this perplexing, as did most of the others. Here was someone experiencing a past life memory about a date in American history that every schoolchild knows. It just didn't make sense. However, having worked for many years in this field, I have learned that the experiences are what they are and should be taken at

---

1. It is important to point out that this work is never guided by my own suggestions. We've all seen entertainment hypnotists make people cluck like a chicken, or take on other behaviors for the amusement of an audience. I assure you that this has no relation to what occurs with past life memory work. The recalling of the experience is always an event of mutual respect and cooperation. I serve as a knowledge guide in the unfolding process of the person's story, assisting in getting to the point where information is useful, rather than just filled with fascinating details.

face value. Since I assumed this woman had no specialized training in early American history, I just let it be.

A couple of days later I was still thinking about what she had said. Aware that Life Memory Recall work can bring extraordinary information to light, I contacted an expert in American history I had met a few years previously. My curiosity had gotten the best of me. I relayed the information as it had been presented in the workshop and asked him to comment.

He flatly replied, "That's correct. The Declaration of Independence was signed on the 2nd and officially dated the 4th."

After thanking him for his time, I hung up the phone with a satisfied smile on my face. I took note of the incident as one more account of how Life Memory Recall works and that the information itself provides its own proof. I learned early on, that the experiences were not for me to define. In this particular incident, it was also an amusing way for the experience to be authenticated.

Although not an example of a healing outcome, this story demonstrates the kind of "real" information that can be retrieved. The mind becomes capable of revealing so much more than we think possible when we choose to be equally accepting of all experiences. This event reaffirmed to me the extraordinary potential of this work when I accept the information as valid. Had I prejudged the information the woman provided simply because I thought it was wrong according to my frame of reference, I would have denied her the truth. Fortunately, it was a truth that would not have affected her one way or the other.

But what if the information could have provided meaning to her quality of life, and accepting the information as real could have resulted in improving her life? This is exactly what occurs for many of my clients. As they expand their definition of what is real, they increase the possibility of finding the information they need to heal. They are no longer limited by their views or the adopted and constrained views of others. Although new views are liberating, they are not that easy to possess.

It is often difficult and challenging to accept another's point of view just because they say so. One way to convince someone of a different way of looking at something is to provide evidence. It is easier to expand or alter your viewpoint when presented with repeatable or undeniable facts. The stories I have been fortunate enough to hear through Life Memory Recall, like the one you are about to read have done this for me.

I was facilitating a workshop for a large gathering at a nearby university. The program started out as it normally would, with preliminary information and a bit of group conversation. I then used my usual regression techniques to elicit a relaxed mood. This opened a doorway for the past life memory experiences to come through. Everyone appeared to be relaxed and calm, and experiencing the usual initial signs that the regression was underway. The process of remembering and recovering a past life proceeded equally well. In this particular workshop, no individual stood out as needing further guidance.

Once I felt the group had satisfactorily accomplished what they came for, I guided them from the regressed state of mind to a more wakeful state. While doing this, I also imparted the usual statement that they would be able to remember their experiences fully. They did and were ready to share. When I opened the floor to discussion, asking who would like to go first, I heard an "Oh, oh!" and a hand went up, energetically waving, like a child who could barely wait to be called on. Of course, I called on her immediately.

To my surprise, what I heard was, "I DIDN'T HAVE ONE. I did not have a past life memory and I am so disappointed. How come I didn't get one?"

"You didn't have one?" I asked.

"No, nothing."

"Nothing?"

"Well…I thought I might have been an Indian, but I'm always reading about Indians."

"What kind of Indian were you?" I asked.

"A Plains Indian, but that is the kind of Indian that I always read about."

"Where did you live?"

"In a teepee, but everyone knows that Plains Indians lived in teepees."

She and I continued recounting the experience in this manner for a short time. To each of my questions, I received a somewhat despondent answer. It was obvious that this woman was convinced that a past life memory had not happened, and whatever did happen had only been the result of recalling what she had read or some form of imagination based on a few facts. I knew better. The hundreds of sessions I encountered prepared me well. I recognized that the conversation was flowing easily, an indication that, although she did not see it herself, we were accessing more and more information about an experience she insisted had never happened. The experience was becoming clearer and clearer. A past life memory was unfolding. The answers would be there.

At one point during the regression, I had asked the group if they could see the supplies they were carrying. I often ask people to look at their surroundings in order to help the visualization process. Again recounting this verbally, I moved to the next question. "Where did you go when I had asked you to go for supplies?"

"I couldn't go for supplies. I was an Indian in the Plains before the white man ever came. Where could I"…her voice trailed off into silence and with surprise in her eyes.

She, along with the rest of us, realized what this last response meant. I had asked her to go for provisions and she could not. She couldn't because there was no place to go in that time period of the past life memory she had experienced. Unlike the previous responses, she had not expected the answer she provided. It was just there. She felt a sense of knowing beyond what she had thought possible, and she felt it confidently. She also realized that something had indeed happened. Her unwillingness to accept the possibility of gathering real information through a past life memory experience faded as she realized the conviction and clarity of her experience.

Had it merely been her imagination, the woman could have easily fabricated a response to satisfy my suggestion. The experience became "real" and seemed authentic when she responded without a preconceived idea of what the answer should be. This demonstrated to her that she was more aware of the experience than she had originally suspected. It convinced her that she had recalled a past life memory rather than her mind's recollection of previously read information. More importantly, there was nothing she had to prove to herself. The experience literally spoke for itself, in a strong and confident voice. There was also nothing the woman had to prove to anyone else. She alone felt the degree to which she experienced the past life memory and it was enough to make it "real".

Interestingly, like the Samurai story in Chapter two, she recovered a past life memory that was of interest in her current life. Had there been more time, could she have found in her experience information that would have been healing, as Carlos had? I cannot say for sure, but I do know that by expanding this woman's definition of what is real, the possibility for using this information as a healing agent was opened. This woman left without limitations and therefore, new possibilities as well.

To assist the process of collecting meaningful information, I have developed a number of methods to enhance the past life memory experience based on my evaluation of the results that have occurred. The greater the healing result, the more carefully I evaluated the past life memory process. My intention was to document any healing outcomes that appeared to be the direct result of the past life memory experience. I was not looking to prove whether past lives were real. I was searching to prove that the memories and information recalled provided for healing results that were real.

I realized this would be difficult to do, as there were no standards of testing on which I could rely. There were no methods to monitor and measure whether a past life memory was an actual event. I could not just matter-of-factly say, "Yes, past life memory is real", even though I personally found the statement to be true. Public opinion on the subject had been varied and the general consensus was that the idea was absurd. This is an opinion that remains fixed in our culture to a large extent, even today.

However, I had support provided by research done in this area of study, and access to the work of credible people who have contributed greatly to a new acceptance of past life work and the value of hypnotherapy.

I would need to follow their lead, although my approach would be different. I would rely on the consistency of the healing results as they were occurring at my workshops and private sessions for the kind of proof I needed. Credibility of Life Memory Recall as a viable mode of healing would come from documented case histories of my work. My obligation is to validate what I already know by using more mainstream methods of research.

So what really occurs during a session before the results are realized and the memory's information becomes real? How people "see" past lives varies with each individual. What doesn't change, however, is each person's own control of the information that comes forward. They, themselves, see and know what they are viewing, and any meaning there is specific to them. It is an experience that is recorded within their minds. The images are clear, concise, and orderly. I simply facilitate the process of bringing the clarity forward when it is not readily understood.

We've all experienced the often confused, strange and disjointed nature of the sleeping dream state. This is not the state Life Memory Recall evokes. Instead, there is a continuity to the vision of a life as it is unfolding under hypnotherapy. The images brought forth contain a logical aware-ness of location, people and/or events. These images may incorporate our other senses. Although a dream can manifest images in a similar fashion, there is a difference. Life Memory Recall work is guided by a facilitator. A person chooses to experience the unfolding images by their own desire, under their own control. A facilitator assists in guiding the process so that the images encountered provide the most meaning.

Whereas dreams have a tendency to unfold haphazardly, this work unfolds with intention. The regressed individual *decides* which way to go or where to go next. Through questioning and response, the facilitator assists in keeping the experience moving forward. The questions help in two ways. First, while the facilitator can only grasp a piece of the experi-ence as it is verbally shared, by listening for responses, he or she can gain insight and clarity into the developing past life experience, and thus assist the individual in increasing their visualization capability should they be "seeing" less than they would wish. In this way, the therapist and client develop a cooperative relationship and the experience is greatly deepened in both detail and content. The therapist and client work together to cre-ate a life picture that becomes a real experience: one that neither fades nor is devoid of useful meaning. Together, information is revealed that may otherwise be left unattended.

For some, the experience takes the form of watching a movie, seeing it as if viewing a screen before them. Others become the main character in the picture created by the mind's eye. They see themselves as an integral part of the landscape, actively participating. When this happens, the individual may exhibit behavior changes appropriate to the scene. For example, changes may occur when an individual is responding to my questions, which manifest as an altered vocal quality or vocabulary. If the person is experiencing a past life as a young child, the responses may become childlike, short and simple in answer, and age appropriate.

During my work with one client, her personality changed with each past life memory. During one session, while recalling a life memory as a child, I asked, "What are you wearing?"

"Jammies," was all she said. Her other responses became similarly monosyllabic and childlike.

In a second one-on-one session, she experienced a past life memory as the ruler of a country. In this case, her tone was completely authoritative and her responses commanding.

In recalling both past life memories, these personality changes helped to make the experience real and immediate for this particular woman. By her definition, the past life memories of the child felt exactly the same as she remembered her current childhood memories. As a ruler, she could relate the change in her tone and general demeanor as a change similar to what she experienced in her daily professional life when it was necessary to assert her authority. To her the experiences presented themselves as if they were occurring in the here and now.

Yet, not everyone has such a dramatic integration between what they "see" and what they externalize. They may not exhibit shifts in personality, but may instead demonstrate more subtle changes. As you read in Carlos' story in chapter 2, an experience may produce verbal cues, incorporating foreign phrases and words not learned during the person's life experiences. Often, these phrases and words can later be translated from the taped session. When the language is real, it is hard to deny that "something" real occurred during the past life memory experience. In other cases, the sentence structure expressed by an individual may change to one used in another time in history; i.e., mannerisms, words, sayings or clichés that have fallen out of common usage. Such was the case with a client who claimed to be of Alaskan origin, an Eskimo. Following the session, which had provided sufficient "language" from the past life memory, I contacted the Native American Language School at the University of Alaska, Fairbanks to have the language evaluated. Their response was that the words and phrases, from an excerpt of the tape I sent to them (with permission from my client), were indeed a native language and that this language was no longer in common usage or from recent times.

I will share another story to further demonstrate these examples. My client was an eighteen year-old girl. We had moved forward in time in her past life memory up to the point where she died in that previous life. When asked what she died from, her response was "consumption." She explained that it was a disease of her lungs and that many people had it. Later, as we discussed the past life memory experience, I asked her if she knew what consumption was. The answer was no. So I explained that consumption was what we now call tuberculosis, and that term was appropriate to the time period of her past life memory. She left my office gratified and with a greater sense of connection to her past life memory and I was pleased to receive more confirmation that while past lives may not necessarily be real or proved to exist, the information they provided always was. While these examples may seem trivial, I've provided them to illustrate how even relatively insignificant details can be important to the person having the past life memory. They become important because they help to open the person to the possibility that something real took place and will likewise support the "realness" of the post-experience effects.

It is important to note that there are other individuals who experience none of the details previously mentioned. For them the authenticity of the experience occurs in other ways. They may not be able to visualize well, and the experience may seem faint or undefined in comparison to the examples above. When this situation occurs, people often express that they feel as though they made the whole thing up. Or they may feel as though creating a picture in their mind's eye was a stretch of their ability to imagine. They feel much less attached to the experience, convinced what little information that did come through came simply from their ability to envision made-up details and the experience's usefulness is questioned. This is when my experience and understanding most effectively comes into play.

In these instances, during the discussion that follows, the retrieved past life memory and its information are put to the test. The more we talk, the more the experience is relived. Added details, initially forgotten, easily begin to flow during the conversation. This is especially notable in group discussions. People will begin to see and feel the experience more fully the more they talk about it. They are usually amazed that the more they verbalize their experience, the more they reveal what they know.

Equally amazing is the change in their perception of what has occurred. As they speak, the details take on meaning. Connections to these details begin to shape the information into a useful form, furnishing a direct correlation to what is happening in their current lives. The information appears insightful. People's faces light up when they realize that the information can be applied to a current life situation that appeared to be a dead-end street. These people become energized by what was provided, empowered by their own ability to shed light when none seemed available. They grasp that they received exactly what they needed, as real as any other experience that moves one forward in the understanding of their lives.

With Life Memory Recall therapy, people get what they need whether they initially know it or not. Whatever happens, however they perceive the experience of recalling a past life memory, there is an effect. For most of the clients these effects are the results they have been searching for. It is a repeated consequence of this work that healing happens, regardless of how the images are initially judged or perceived. Whether the experience is visual, auditory, tactile, kinesthetic or just sensed and felt, the experience has a positive effect on the current events in one's life. This is about as real as an experience can get.

We now know that the experiences and information provided by this therapy are real, based on the understanding that it is made real by the results that occur. But, can we also know that a past life memory itself is real? Can the recalling of a past life experience be verified, proven to exist? We need to consider the definition of a past life memory by exploring a few more pertinent questions before trying to definitively answer.

First, do we all have past lives? For many people, the idea of the existence of past lives is contrary to what has been taught by their culture, tradition or religion. They may view this concept as, at best, nonsense and at worst, heretical. The process of Life Memory Recall would be unacceptable if it demanded a belief in reincarnation (the recycling of our soul from one body life to another). Fortunately, it does not. The ability to experience a past life memory does not require a change in belief.

The next obvious question then becomes, if it's not reincarnation, what is it?

A past life memory is, in its most basic form, a visual representation. It is what the mind brings forth during a state of complete relaxation when it is freed to wander. The images come together to form a life picture complete with shapes and surroundings that may or may not be similar to normal daily life experiences. The person having the experience never loses sight of who they are or where they are, they simply suspend making judgments about the images they are experiencing. In this state of non-judgment, the mind is allowed to expand further, increasing the ability to visualize without restriction. A personality takes form, complete with a time and place.

The images are no longer random visions, but come together to create a story. In most cases, these stories are considered past events or lives since they are chronologically identified with a time in past human history.[2] The stories are about earlier times, places, events and even locations. They can be from the very distant past as well as recent past. For example, a person or people in the past life memories behave according to whatever time period is chosen and are also costumed accordingly. There is often a

---

2. Because of this, you will find the terms Life Memory Recall and past life memory used interchangeably throughout this book without the need to validate the experience as either distant past, recent past or moments earlier in a current life.

wealth of detail, exactly as one would expect when reading any other kind of story.

Unexpectedly, information can emerge from these sessions that would not be readily accessible by any other means. A vantage point is created that allows a person the gift of a new, less limited perspective, creating a source for deeper personal meaning. The fact that these experiences exist is enough to give credence to the concept that an individual can and does tap into hidden wisdom that is revealed in the form of a human experience. Therefore, it is not necessary to believe in reincarnation or the actual recycling of life to believe that the image of a human life can be retrieved. This is fortunate, because it provides freedom from judgment, allowing for noninterference with any beliefs held by culture, tradition or religion. The past life memory may be accepted, by definition, as real imaginings of the mind that provide information with potential meaning for a person's current life situations; information that presents itself as a past life experience.

Are there any other explanations for these experiences? The answer is yes. In the many years of doing this work and the research for this book, a number of other explanations have been suggested.

One very plausible explanation has been provided by scientific study of the human brain, and the conclusion that we humans are aware of much more than we realize. It poses the question, what occurs in the approximately 90 percent of unknown and uncharted gray matter between our ears? Do the answers to unexplainable phenomena rest in the recesses of the unmapped convolutions of our brain tissue? These questions and more have opened the door of experimentation and launched a search for answers.

One example of this is the search for what makes intelligence. This query alone has led to some interesting studies. One of these was the preservation of Albert Einstein's brain, kept in order to study what made his intellectual capacity so great. Although the physiologic study matters, what has mattered most to the majority of us is what his intelligence meant; how his intelligence or knowing affected himself and others. He was not afraid of being called a fool for believing in the information and knowledge he possessed. It was real to him no matter how unbelievable it appeared to others. Realizing the truth of his findings, allowing them to be expressed, he changed our entire worldview. He did this without needing to immediately validate his beliefs about the knowledge he had. He just believed in his own experience and understanding. This is to some degree how Life Memory Recall works. It is a method to change the individual's view by allowing information that may appear to come from an unknown or non-defined source the freedom to surface. Like Einstein's information, it may be unusual compared to the present understanding yet when not judged it can generate a whole new world of possibilities. Like Einstein's information, tests to validate its "realness" will be required to help prove the new possibilities and this will take time and innovation.

However the unexplainable experiences or events or sources are tested, conclusions may remain controversial, nonexistent, or just plain mysterious. Such is the situation regarding Extrasensory Perception or ESP. There are years worth of data from study after study, yet, not one acceptable conclusion has ever been reached. Psychic phenomenon such as intuition, clairaudience, clairvoyance, clairsentience, and premonition, to name just a few, are included in this category. The only reasonable conclusion we can draw is that when studying the brain and its extraordinary feats, there may be no unreputable answer. Indeed, what this may suggest is that our testing methods have been unsuitably designed for the subjects. In a world where science looks toward empirical evidence for validating results, these circumstances may exist well out of the range of current human understanding. Nonetheless, it is clear that phenomena exist that have been proven worthy of scientific attention. Why? Because there is a real outcome; an effect as a result of some experience.

This is the case with Life Memory Recall. There are currently no instruments to test and measure whether our bodies, our personalities or our essences have been recycled, lifetime after lifetime. Nor can we prove if it is possible to recall them at will. Equally difficult to prove, is where the information in our brain actually comes from. We are left with a partial explanation, neither affirming nor denying that a past life experience occurs as a result of an unknown brain function. If this definition fits an individual's belief system better than the concept of reincarnation, then it should be accepted. As long as a person is not impeded by his or her beliefs, they will have as great an opportunity as any to experience this work and gain access to the relevant meaning it evokes.

A third explanation, presenting an even greater challenge of proof, is based on the theory called cellular memory[3]. An offshoot of genetic research, it contends that human beings pass on more information within our genetic code than merely the chromosomes that direct our growth as a species. Science, having mapped with functional understanding about three percent of our DNA, calls the remaining ninety-seven percent "junk DNA". The human genome project concluded that although complete maps can be created, the work of understanding the meaning of how our DNA and genes function is the stuff of future science. It is with a focus on the unknown and unexplored portions of our DNA that some unusual theories have been recently presented. No matter how bizarre or unbelievable they seem, they should not be dismissed as unworthy of study.

The theory of cellular memory does not rely on DNA mapping alone. Instead, it came about by combining biological theories with modern physics. The idea of cellular memory works on the assumption that we are not only a biological system, but an energy system as well. It suggests that both components are involved in the communication between each cell. Further, it suggests that information is passed from cell to cell, which in turn affects the entire body and is stored within our DNA, possibly the duty of the so-called "junk" genes. This information includes our thoughts. Because they are the products of a bioelectrical reaction, they are part biology and part energy. The further implication is that every thought can be communicated either chemically or electrically to every cell and is, in fact, a part of its make-up.

If this proves true, then what does it imply with regard to the passing on of information through the procreative process? Does this mean that every thought I have ever had may be stored and then passed on to my children?

---

3. More information on the theory of cellular memory can be found in the work of Gary E. Schwartz, Ph.D, a professor of Psychology, Medicine, Neurology, Psychiatry and Surgery, and Director of the VERITAS Research program at the University of Arizona.

Could this represent a process that makes the ability to remember past lives a fact of one's biology?

There is absolutely no way to know for sure. There are additional theories more far reaching than those already briefly mentioned with respect to expanding our ideas of what is possible. That leaves us with a wide range of possibilities from which to choose how we want to interpret the past life memory experience. It also means that whatever explanation you accept as a theory to authenticate past life memory work, you cannot be wrong! Nor will the information recalled be made less real in meaning as a result of the explanation chosen. The experience remains real, because the information clearly exists and "real" effects as a result can be witnessed.

A few possible explanations of the why's and how's of past life memory have been briefly explored. Like the good scientist who makes a hypothesis and then tests that hypothesis, I have spent a great deal of time testing my own theories. For me personally, my acceptance came following an encounter with a client who later became my colleague. During our sessions, Hollie provided me with yet another theory that caused me to question my own definition of what was real as it pertained to past life experiences. Her theory was broad enough in scope to encompass all of the theories discussed above as truth and presented the possibility that even more unknown or undefined information could exist as well.

We taped session after session retrieving more information, until all the pieces fit together more tightly than any puzzle I have ever seen. Together, as we tested hers, now our theory, dramatic changes in results occurred instantaneously. My clients began experiencing profound changes immediately following the remembrance of their past lives. While the information had felt real enough before, as had the past life experience in most cases, the results were now quite different. People were healing in ways I had not seen before. And while the level of healing had deepened, so too had the speed of recovery. People were getting better in all kinds of ways, their problems and dis-eases improved rapidly. This means that something much more profound than expected was happening. In light of these new results, any limitations I had previously placed on the definition of a past life memory, the process of Life Memory Recall, the value of the information, or the reason for the results were completely erased.

Hollie's theory, when I applied it, had a positive effect on the results I was getting with my clients, but even more important was the effect it had on my work. It brought clarity to twenty years of sometimes confusing and conflicting information by showing me how all the pieces fit together. It changed the way I thought. What I had once thought unbelievable became possible. This theory will be revealed to you in the chapters that follow, by telling Hollie's story and our story together as it happened.

For now, it is important to know that as I changed, so did the techniques and definition of my work. New names for the experiences were required which could incorporate my expanded view. I was no longer a Past Life Regression therapist. Instead I was becoming a "This Life Therapist". My work became as much about a person's current life as it was about past lives. I saw that there is a connectedness between the two. This is how Life Memory Recall came into being. Later, expanding on this newly found concept came the development of a technique called: Guided Light Therapy. Both names by design leave the door open for personal interpretation, neither strictly defined nor limited by any particular belief system. Additionally, the delineation between past and present has evaporated into a single continuum of support. Although the techniques have a definite structure, their names reflect their unlimited range. Also unlimited are the results I am seeing, some of which I have shared in this book.

Sharing the stories of people who have been helped by this method will provide you with the information you need to answer the question, "Is this for real?" In answering, you may also discover new meaning for your own life path. It may lead you, as it has many of my clients, toward a healing result.

The work that lies ahead must focus on providing the evidence that the results of Life Memory Recall work is healing, and that the results are repeatable. This means first finding a satisfactory definition of what constitutes healing. To fully understand the Life Memory Recall process, we must consider the following questions: "How do we define healing?" and "What kinds of healing are possible?"

Chapter 4

▼

Common Sufferings

Once it was established that healing was actually taking place, only a few thoughts away and a few steps ahead was the question of *what* could be healed? Until now, the physical healing effects experienced by people I had worked with were reported on an "Oh, by the way…" basis, almost as side effects. They were happy and I was happy, too. However, as my technique changed, the healing results desired began occurring with more speed and consistency. People called or wrote to me, often almost immediately after their session, telling me how quickly things were positively changing for them.

Looking more critically at the process, the first stages of a preliminary analysis began. I decided that the most straightforward approach to evaluating the surprisingly accelerated and more obvious healing effects would be through the exploration of the effects of the work on common problems. In addition to concentrating on the behavioral and/or emotional healing the method was initially intended to provide, I began to pay attention to the physical healing that was also taking place. A similarity emerged in the way the process worked, no matter the current condition. The illness or the perception of dis-ease was altered, making all aspects important and worthy of investigation. The range of the work and its healing capabilities were expanding, along with the consistency of results.

The true scope of healing that may be achievable with this method is yet unknown. What is known is that there exists a body of results that indicate that "real" healing has taken place, healing that is measurable by current methods. The only limitations that I have found to date are the limitations of my own beliefs. Therefore, I have never turned away anyone who has sought healing, regardless of his or her current condition, problem or state of dis-ease. In turn, I offer a process of healing that, on first glance, may seem simply unbelievable. I do not guarantee that the method will work as they desire, but rather, that it has helped others receive exactly what they needed. With this understanding going in, my clients and I explore new realms of possibility, which can be especially useful and important for those who have had less than successful results with previous healing methods.

Because misconceptions about this work and its potential for healing are common, it is important to offer stories of healing that link to commonly encountered chronic problems or illnesses. There are certain common afflictions that affect just about everyone, either directly or indirectly through someone that they know. First, I will tell you the story of a woman with arthritis. Then, later on in this chapter, I will address a problem that has continuously found its way to my office; weight problems and the effects of eating disorders.

I was giving a workshop on a typical early spring evening in New England. The night was chilly and rainy, with a penetrating dampness. At this workshop I noticed a young girl who was walking with a cane. During one of the breaks, I approached her and asked if she had injured herself. She told me that during the past couple of years she had developed early onset arthritis. The arthritis had affected all of her joints from her neck to her feet. She consulted her family physician as well as an arthritis specialist. After their evaluation, they remained puzzled. The type of arthritis she was exhibiting normally happened in the later stages of life and was not a type that should be occurring in someone so young. Yet, here it was.

Although she had used traditional methods to alleviate her condition, the ailment continued to plague her. She had really good days and some not so good days. On particularly bad days, she told me, she was known to use a cane. That evening the cold dampness had made it a "bad" day.

I had worked with people with arthritis before, and the results had been positive, although, until now I dealt more with pain management than actually working toward a significant change in the condition itself. However, through my research on the results my clients were receiving, my technique had evolved to a point where I was prepared to suggest that Life Memory Recall could do more than heal the emotional response and help with the management of this awful condition. It was with this in mind that I discussed my beliefs with "Jennifer". I expressed to her that the range of possible healing by this technique was not as limited as I had originally believed. I explained my belief that changes in a person's physical condition were possible following the experience of encountering a past life memory when the past life memory found its connection to a current life situation. I also told her that how this process worked was still unknown, and expressed the simple statements "It appears that when the mind is open and free to explore, it will seek the answers for itself, the result of which can have an extreme impact on the desired outcome. Regardless of obtaining or not obtaining healing results, information useful for her current condition would be retrieved and revealed."

Although she had found various forms of relief, Jennifer dreaded the thought of living with a condition that she was told would most probably only get worse. At 20, this had been the hardest part for her. Impressed with the fact that I seemed so convinced that some helpful information would come, and satisfied with my explanation of the technique, Jennifer stated that she was willing to try. If nothing else, she thought, maybe she could at least find a way to feel better about her proposed fate. With this in mind, we began. I have edited our session to include just the pertinent details for the convenience of the reader.

"What do you see? What do you see on the ground?" I questioned.

"Fields."

"Describe them to me."

"Fields, green, stone walls, trees in the distance, a dirt path."

"Do you see yourself?"

"Yeah."

"How old are you, and what are you wearing?"

"I'm 20. I'm wearing pants. Old linen shirt."

"What is your name?"

"Robert. Robert Bard, I'm in Scotland."

It is a common aspect of Life Memory Recall to have the individual identify a specific name associated with a past life memory. It is equally common to have the subject's gender in the past life memory change from their current life status. When referring to my client, I routinely use the name given during a session when I am questioning and searching for the useful information this technique provides. It's important to note that at no time is the person experiencing the past life memory unaware of his/her true self. It is easier, however, for the person recalling a past life to obtain more vivid images by my using the name given for the particular memory.

"Do you know what year it is, Robert? Do you know where around in Scotland you are?" I continued.

"16…1630. North Country."

"What do you do Robert?"

"Take care of the sheep. I'm supposed to be taking care of the sheep and I'm not."

"What are you doing?"

"Going fishing. Yeah, I'm going fishing."

"What's happening to the sheep?"

Robert chuckles lightly after the asking of this question and says, "I tricked my little brother into taking care of them. He's going to be mad, but I'm having a good time."

In order to enhance the past life memory, I began a line of questioning that allowed greater detail to emerge. He was living in a small village. Both of his parents were alive. Robert was unmarried and living at home in order to help take care of the family farm. He had one younger brother, the very brother he had tricked into taking care of the sheep. A few other details surfaced until it was time to proceed with the session to a point in this past life where Robert could retrieve information that applied to his current situation.

"Robert, when I make a noise with my fingers, go to a point in your life that will have some relationship to the arthritis you have now, okay?"

"Yeah."

"How old are you now?"

"35."

"What is the relationship to your arthritis?"

"Very, very cold."

"Where is it cold?" I inquired. At this point in the session, I could see Jennifer's body becoming stiff and tight, as though she was freezing. She also began to shiver. The memory of Robert Bard and the associated past life was having an effect on Jennifer in the present. It was as if Robert's experience was becoming Jennifer's, which could now be obviously seen while we delved into the experience for deeper meaning. In no way, however, was Jennifer truly uncomfortable while recalling the past life memory.

"It's very cold in the water."

"Why are you in the water?"

"For diving."

"What are you diving for?"

"There's snow. The ice is frozen. There is a hole in the ice."

"What do you do with the hole in the ice?"

"Someone fell."

"Someone fell in? Who fell in? Who fell in, Robert?"

"Jimmy, my little brother."

"What did you try to do? Save him?"

"Yeah."

"Were you successful?"

"No. We're looking...we're looking for the body...to bury. He's not alive."

"Why did he fall in? What did he do?"

"He was walking across the lake and fell in, for some reason, I don't know why. It was weak and it just...", Robert's voiced faded away without finishing his response.

"What does this have to do with your arthritis?"

"I feel it is my fault."

"Your fault that he fell in? Is that what you feel?"

"Yes. I'm the older brother." An audible sigh followed this response.

"Will you explain this?" I asked. At this point, my question was leading but not commanding. As a facilitator of this work, it is important to act as a guide, as I mentioned earlier. By asking the question in this way, the person experiencing the memory creates whatever is needed without being influenced in any way by the facilitator. The information found must be free of any suggestion in order for it to have the significance and meaning that remains uniquely individual. In this way, its future application for the person and his/her current condition remains directly linked. An ownership of the experience becomes necessary later when it is time to release the past experience, which in turn releases any ties this past experience has to the present.

Robert continued, "My mother and father are going to be very upset...disappointed."

"Your arthritis is from the guilt?"

The answer was an undeniable 'yes'. In our discussion following this session, Jennifer expressed that she felt she had held onto guilt from feeling responsible for his (her) little brother, Jimmy's death. This paralyzing guilt felt centuries old to her, and stemmed from the fact that he (she) was too lazy to do what his mother had asked and the result was carried within Jennifer. As she recalled the cold, stiff feelings in her body as a result of the dive into the lake, we were both fascinated how the feelings from her past life memory were much the same as what her body was now experiencing. So we questioned, by releasing this memory, would her symptoms also be released? Would she now experience relief from the frozen emotions caused by an inner guilt? And could the release of this guilt release the locked feelings in her joints now?

I asked Jennifer to call me and let me know if there were any changes in her arthritis following the recovery and release of this past life memory. She kindly agreed.

In the weeks ahead, I did not hear from her as promised. I did not know how effective the past life remembrance was, or for that matter, if it had helped her or not.

It was three years later when I finally received a letter from Jennifer. By this time, I had almost forgotten about her session. The letter was a revelation. Jennifer wrote that on the day following our session she no longer needed her cane. She stated, "I am happy to say that today I don't even know what happened to the cane." She had also stopped taking the medications she was on to ease her discomfort, since the pain had dissipated also.

She continued, "As I write the above account, the memory of that past life is still with me very clearly. I hesitated to write this for you, Norton, as you asked three years ago. Although at the time I seemed to have no further symptoms of arthritis, I wanted to be sure that this affliction was truly gone. Today, I can honestly say that I have no trace of the arthritis in my body."

I have spoken to Jennifer a number of times since receiving her letter. As wonderful as the amazing recovery detailed in her letter was, what has happened since is even more remarkable. Today, no longer plagued by the arthritic symptoms of a few years earlier and free of medications, Jennifer is now a kickboxing instructor with a black belt in karate! Quite the change from when we first met.

Jennifer's story demonstrates the profound connections that can occur with Life Memory Recall. Yet, we need to question whether this was a unique case of healing. It was without a doubt, almost miraculous, considering the present changes she experienced in her current condition. Often, it is through these stories that we are left in awe of the process, yet, can also feel detached from them because of their extraordinary circumstances and associated outcomes. Simply stated, it's hard to believe that such changes can and do take place. Often the response to these kinds of healing stories is one of separation, and the question, "Why them and not me?" Or as I hear too commonly, "Miracles are for a few chosen people, not for me." It is then that I ask, "Why *not* you?"

My work with the technique has allowed me to explore this question. It has opened a window wide enough for me to believe that healing results are possible given any circumstance, for anyone. Just as some traditional methods may produce different results for different people, so too is the nature of past life memory experiences. Not all people that come to me receive the kind of instantaneous physical results that Jennifer received. The majority do however, experience some type of healing results. This is true because healing results achieved through this technique are not limited to the physical body. More often than not, a physical problem is also associated with psychological, behavioral, emotional and even spiritual problems. When the information brought forth by a past life memory heals any of these other aspects of a dis-ease, the possibility for physical changes follows, although not always manifested. This comprehensive view and expanded understanding of the interconnectedness of healing possibilities was made available by working with Hollie. It is but one example of how my beliefs changed after we met. It is also an example of how far reaching healing changes could be when doing past life memory work. I learned that any change of the past creates a change in the present, and sometimes these changes come in miraculous ways and sometimes in ways less dramatic or obvious than in Jennifer's story. Yet the fact remains that a healing of some kind has occurred and a life has been improved. This represents the unlimited range available through this work.

The following stories will serve to better demonstrate what I mean. The chronic problems of weight control and eating disorders have always presented themselves as reasons that someone would seek my help. This occurred earlier in my career when I was conducting stress management courses, and was just as prevalent in my later work with Life Memory Recall. Given its continual presence, I was not surprised when I heard a statistic that one in every four girls in the U.S. has some type of eating disorder. It is a common ailment in my work and prevalent enough to merit my full attention.

I received a call from a young girl who had graduated from college a few years earlier and had the eating disorder known as bulimia. Until the time of her call, she had been able to hide the disorder from everyone. However, it had progressed recently to the point where she could not hide it any longer and was therefore, searching for any means to help. She had heard about the work I was doing and was willing to give it a try.

We set up the first appointment shortly after our phone conversation. A girl in her early twenties, she was attractive, laughed effortlessly and had an engaging smile. At about five feet, three or four inches tall, I noted that she appeared average in stature, neither tall nor short. More noticeable to me, given the nature of the problem that brought her to see me, her weight appeared equally normal, if not also average for someone her size. Basically, she did not look heavy or undernourished, nor did she have the appearance of the classical look of an anorexic or bulimic individual whose disorder was fully integrated into their lives. I became intrigued, mostly because of her *normal* appearance, to hear her story.

The young woman, whom I will call Ashley, said that she had been bulimic for the past six years starting about the time she was a sophomore in college. She was a bright student and was very aware of the health problems that could result from bulimia. Because Ashley was aware, her management of her bulimic condition included making prudent choices in order to limit some of the potential health risks associated with this condition.

She had a constant driving need to eat and fill her stomach. She said she was always hungry and always felt that she had to eat more. Instead of eating whatever she could, it was in this regard that she made choices in accordance with some nutritional understanding. She never ate cakes, cookies, ice cream or other foods that were fat-laden or contained high amounts of refined carbohydrates. Rather, she would eat large quantities of low calorie foods or vegetables. This could, at first glance, appear to be a well-constructed diet of sound nutritional value. However, Ashley took it to an extreme. She could and did eat five pounds of carrots a day, along with a couple of pounds of string beans and/or a pot of cooked broccoli. She did this so often, that in her last year of college, she reported that her skin turned a slight orange. There was enough color that her friends wanted to know if she had gone to Florida or the Bahamas during their winter break, assuming that she had gotten a tan. Embarrassed, she would reply that she was eating too many carrots and it was a result of the carotene causing a temporary pigmentation in her skin. This was the first indication that hiding her bulimia was getting harder.

Second to the "managed" diet was Ashley's attempts to control the purging associated with bulimia. Always aware and worried about the health risks of her condition, Ashley eliminated the need to vomit or use suppositories through compulsive exercise. She would run several miles each day along with performing aerobic routines. If she couldn't run or move about while she exercised, she would do it while staying in one place.

Up until she came to see me, Ashley felt she had managed her disorder reasonably well. Now, she felt she could no longer control her eating. She found herself maintaining a normal eating pattern in public, but when no one was left to watch, usually once everyone was asleep, she would spend literally a couple of hours eating. While she was continuing to consume a large amount of vegetables, she now ate anything that she could, including breads, cakes, or cookies. She binged on whatever was in the house.

When Ashley finished explaining her condition, I explained my technique to her. She understood that we would together, in a relaxed or light hypnotic state where she could feel safe and comfortable, search for possible connections for her bulimic tendencies from her past. The following is an excerpt from our taped session. We begin at the point where Ashley encounters a past life memory.

"I think I am in an oriental country. I think it is Cambodia. There is a small baby. The baby is screaming. She is hungry." Ashley continued her description until I had the impression that she was a relatively young woman who was the mother of the baby, still an infant.

"Can you feed her?" I asked. "Can you give her some milk from your breast? Can you get milk of any kind to feed the baby?"

"She (referring to the young Cambodian mother) does not have any milk. She had other children. They are little. She does not have enough to eat and cannot make milk for the baby. There is no place to get milk."

Then Ashley tells me that the mother is giving the baby her breast but there is nothing there. The baby continues to cry and there is nothing for it to eat. After this explanation, Ashley reverts back to speaking as if the young mother is speaking and says, "The baby does not live very long. The baby dies. The other children are weak, but they are living."

After a brief pause, Ashley continued, "I cannot do anything for them. I tried and tried."

A second pause ensued before Ashley said, "We just keep walking."

"Where are you going?"

"Anywhere. Anywhere we can get food. Everyone is also walking and looking. There is just nothing.

"Where are you and what year is it?"

"Cambodia," said Ashley, then, speaking as if she were an observant bystander, "She is also hungry, but she doesn't care. She is concerned about the children. She has not eaten for days so she no longer feels the hunger, it has gone away. For her children, she does not want the hunger to stop as much as she wants their crying to stop. She is being so good, but there is nothing that she [we] can do. Walking and carrying whatever we have. Always looking for food."

"What are you looking for?"

"Want rice, milk, just rice. Everything is so dry. It is too swampy for the rice to grow here."

Again Ashley interrupted the direct conversation to give another report. She informed me that the woman has lost another child. It had died and, shortly after, another died too. The scene remained similar. At this point in the session I moved Ashley ahead a couple of years in order to facilitate a forward momentum toward the meaning of this memory. She informed me that only two of the five children, the older ones, had survived.

Ashley stated, "We go to a city. We are in a small room. Tries to give the kids whatever she can. They are surviving."

"How well are you surviving?" I inquired.

"Not well."

"Do you get enough to eat?"

"No. Whatever I make I give to the kids."

"How do you make money?"

She spoke now in a hushed, almost inaudible voice "It is embarrassing. The only thing I have to sell is me."

"What country are you in and what year is it?" To this question, Ashley responded that it was Cambodia or possibly a part of Vietnam. She thinks the year is 1967. After hearing this, I asked if she was ready to go to the point in that life when she died.

"Let's, please!" This plea surprised me, until I realized that she was looking forward to death in that life. So we went quickly to the point of her death. She died in her late thirties. I then asked, "What did you die from?"

"Lack of energy. The older children are still alive."

"Do you go right up (*into the light*)?"[1] My experience with this work has demonstrated time and again that people often see themselves staying around after their deaths to see how their children and family are after they have crossed over. Ashley answered that she stayed for a while. In the end, the two older children were all right. It was a struggle, but they made it.

It was time to assist Ashley with gaining meaning from her experience, so I proceeded by asking what lesson she had to learn and did she learn that lesson?

"It all has to do with food." Ashley began to cry.

I guided Ashley back to a place where she felt warm and peaceful. We went further into this place, allowing her to release the grief of her past life memory about food. We worked together until Ashley was sure that what was in the past would remain in the past. Her only connection to it now was her ability to be able to let go of the past life memory of starvation. She would retain this lesson and understand with new meaning that it would no longer be a part of her current life. Upon releasing this memory to remain in the past, the session ended, with Ashley feeling relieved, happy, loved, and well. Before we closed our session, I asked if there were any other past memories related to her eating disorder. We concluded that

---

1. In the later chapters of this book this concept will be explored as the technique of *Guided Light Therapy* is explained. For now, it need only be explained as necessary given the nature of Ashley's life memory.

while there may be, it was the life in Cambodia that was the main reason for the emergence of the eating disorder today.

A few weeks later, I found out how Ashley was doing after our session. She related to me that the first night, she ate her evening meal and left food on her plate, something she rarely did. For the first time in years, she was able to stop eating when she was no longer hungry, and she was free of the desire to eat beyond her hunger. Once the hunger from the experience of the young Cambodian mother was released, so too was Ashley's insatiable desire for food. More than this, Ashley expressed that she no longer worried about her bingeing or purging, and that she no longer felt gripped by her need to spend hours a day exercising. She added more foods to her diet. Her life had shifted into a more normal pattern, including a regained sense of inner control. Instead of the preoccupation with food, she was beginning to use her time productively.

It has been over three years since Ashley came to me with her problem of bulimia and unique eating patterns. She now eats when she is hungry and stops when she is full. She eats what she wants, when she wants, without any need for hiding how she eats because her eating habits are normal, so normal, in fact, that she told me she has maintained the same dress size since she left the starving Cambodian woman and her five children behind. The bingeing and purging did indeed become a memory of her past.

Ashley's disorder was extreme and her results extraordinary, which makes her story both unique and fascinating. Yet, what about problems less severe? Can Life Memory Recall work on these too? The answer is that I have had similar success with other related, but less extreme eating problems. While healing stories of profound changes are always gripping, I believe an equal consideration of less severe, more common problems is just as significant. As an example, I share the following story about weight loss.

Weight loss may seem to many to be a simple thing or a minimal problem. However, if you are the person experiencing difficulty losing weight, you know how disturbing this can be. Weight control can be a life long battle for some, and therefore, can have profound effects on a person's life when healed.

Life Memory Recall can be used for the person for whom the process of losing weight is not so simple. These people may require more than a calorie restricted diet, a decrease of fattening foods or an 'eat less/exercise more' program. They may have tried simple hypnosis to curb the desire for extra calories, to ease away from junk foods or to add exercise to a daily routine, without success. Life Memory Recall may provide successful results for those who have tried all the routine routes, including various methods of motivation or suggestion, and yet have not experienced the results they are searching for.

I have used the technique for clients who had tried to control their weight with diet and exercise, with only frustratingly temporary success. There were people who constantly had a desire or need to eat, who never experienced the sensation of fullness, leading to an insatiable appetite with a never diminishing impulse to eat. My professional experience has demonstrated repeatedly that these individuals will not be helped completely by diet and exercise alone or by simple hypnotic suggestion. For these individuals the root of the problem beyond the physical must be found.

There is also the person who eats very little, yet whose bodies seem to hang onto every calorie they eat. Where another person may eat celery for a few days and lose a couple of pounds, they seem to gain it. I have heard from individuals who face such a situation jokingly say that they can gain weight just by watching someone else eat. Not funny at all, if you are the individual who struggles with this unreasonable dilemma. No matter what they seem to do, the weight is never fully shed.

These, along with other examples of the variety of weight problems people face, have proven to be more similar than dissimilar in one important way. I have discovered that there appears to be a common thread that is linked to the success or failure of an individual's desired result. This is best served by the cliché, *Losing weight may not be what you eat, but what is eating you!* In past life memory work, I have found this statement proven true time and again, and it uncovers a need for a deep-seated healing that far transcends the effectiveness of diet, exercise, or other types of behavior modification. By heading back into one's past to discover the reason for the weight gain and retention of weight, the problem generally is solved. Once the problem is discovered and released, the weight problem disappears.

It is important to note that I have indulged here in a bit of an oversimplification, because Life Memory Recall has also revealed that once the cause is found, achieving the desired results may require not only a release of the past experience, but a need for current life changes that many may be unwilling or unable to make. Unlike most traditional therapies for weight control where the emphasis is on one's biology, behavior, or mental state, Life Memory Recall often reveals an underlying emotional link related to the cause of a weight problem. If changes are not made, the healing results may be limited to some degree.

This next story demonstrates what I mean about the emotional link to weight. One individual came to me for a simple hypnosis session to lose weight. We had two sessions before I followed up with him. He had lost some weight, although it was very little. I called a second time shortly after the first phone call. He said he had not lost one pound. I asked him to come back one more time, explaining that there was a non-traditional process I felt sure would work for him.

When he returned, I explained about the possibility that there could be something in his past that was preventing him from losing the desired weight. We talked about past life regression, and I mentioned that it had the potential to solve this individual's weight problem. Once he agreed to try it, we proceeded with the regression work, and discovered a significant past life memory.

It was in the 1400's in a southern European country, and the memory encountered was a life as a female. One day while going through a wooded area on an errand for her mother, a man attacked her and she was raped. As we explored this experience, the rape did not seem to affect the girl's life at that time. She eventually got married and had a pretty ordinary and good life. She was not heavy in that life. However, a link was made between that life and the current one.

My client reacted as if he were the woman who was raped, reacting emotionally. He described the need to put on weight for protection, in order to be unappealing. The fear of being victimized remained, although in a different form. As the man released the past experience[2], he could clearly see the connection he was carrying from a past life memory and his life now. He had put on weight and kept it on, and here was his link to why he could not get rid of it. I realize that this may sound contrived or the connection made up, however, to my client there was a personal and powerful emotional attachment to the recalled past life memory. And this is what is important, remembering that Life Memory Recall therapy works with meaning on the individual level and therefore does not require validation of the "realness" of the connection such as the one in this man's story. What matters is the end result.

After a few weeks had passed, I received a phone call from this man to let me know how he was doing. He was pleased to report that he had lost seven pounds over the past two weeks. This was no small change to someone who had tried many other attempts at weight loss without success. It was a big step in the right direction. For this he was pleased and agreed to call me again in a month or so. True to his word, he did. This time, there was much more excitement in his voice. He proceeded to tell me that his eating habits had not changed much, but nonetheless, he had now lost over twenty pounds, and was still losing weight. He said that having had the past life memory experience and realizing his ability to release it, he also had no reason to hold onto the extra weight. It could be released, too.

While this connection may sound odd or even preposterous, more times than not, it is exactly this kind of a link that is created by past life work which allows for changes to occur in an individual's current situation. Rarely, in the case of weight management, is there *not* an underlying cause beyond inappropriate eating habits or the lack of an exercise regimen. If the cause is not found and released, it can continue to exacerbate and aggravate the eating problem.

---

2. The concept of releasing a past life memory will be described in greater detail in later chapters. Generally, it means to no longer feel attached to the memory in any way; a process of letting go.

Another common theme related to weight and past life memories are experiences retrieved relating to starvation, either the starvation of the individual, as in Ashely's case, or concerning guilt over causing another to go hungry. Such was the case with another person who came to see me for weight control. What was unique is that the experience rediscovered was much more recent than either of us had assumed. Unlike past life regression, Life Memory Recall, as it has been developed, includes all past experiences up to the present moment. This expanded view of regression therapy is in fact, exactly why the process came into being. A past life memory, from this process, can be referring to someone's childhood in the current life as easily as it could refer to the life of a child hundreds of years ago.

For the individual who came to me about a weight problem, it was a past life memory from his youth in his current life that had been forgotten, yet was emotionally affecting his behavior now. As we explored his past together, a child's life memory came forward.

He told me he had grown up in a very poor family. While the children's basic needs were taken care of, and they received sufficient amounts of food to not go hungry, only the barest of essentials were provided. There were no extras, such as desserts or special items to look forward to. They never went out for an ice cream cone or purchased anything beyond bread from the local bakery. Often, the children in this family would see their friends enjoy candy, cakes, cookies and other sweets. For this person in particular, he felt envious most of the time. He felt he had missed an important element of his childhood.

As he became older and was working on his own, he vowed that he would be compensated and would make up for all the things he did not have as a child. He remembered the first time he went grocery shopping on his own. He was pushing a cart down the cereal aisle when he realized how many there were and that there were children's "fun" cereals. The type of cereals he could never have had in his youth. Further, he realized he could now afford to buy whatever he wanted. So he did. He began to catch up on all the foods he missed. However, over time he did more than catch up, he never stopped. He kept feeding himself everything he was deprived of in order to make up for what went unfilled earlier. Until he came to do Life Memory Recall work, there was no way to release him from this feeling.

We went back to the earlier time in his childhood. Through this process he was able to be the deprived child once again. He could now look at this child who wanted so much to be like everyone else and have what others had. He discovered that the emotional cause was deeper than he had expected, and in ways that related to more than a lack of certain foods. The child had used food to express his dissatisfaction with his family situation. The extras in life that this small child craved, yet was denied, was represented by the desserts and sweets his family could not afford. This came as a surprise to this man. He now clearly understood why he was eating these particular foods and why he couldn't seem to stop. The realization was good, but it would not be enough to stop this behavior until the actual memory was released. The releasing is as important an aspect of the Life Memory Recall process as the recalling of the life experience itself.

While regressed, this individual was able to retrieve the experience while now seeing it from his adult perspective. He was able to release the strong childhood frustrations and desires that affected him presently. He was able to do so because he could realize that these frustrations were not needed any longer in his adult life. He made the connections between his emotional need to eat and his habitual need to eat in a manner that would help him regain his health. Additionally, he healed in another way. He had overcome his childhood woes. The possibility to heal did not occur until this realization had been brought forward as it was in the past life memory experience. Prior to our session together, this gentleman had not known the origin of his eating problem or how to get rid of it. Worse, he did not know that he had some internal pain left over since his childhood.

By the time I saw him again, he had lost a considerable amount of weight. He told me he found it easier to avoid eating the amount of junk food he used to eat. While he does still have an occasional dessert or sweet, his view of having them has changed. No longer a compulsion of need, they now represented something to be enjoyed on a special occasion. Through the past life memory technique, once the cause was isolated, this individual was released from the drive to fill himself, no longer compensating for the feelings of a deprived child long ago grown up.

In each case mentioned in this chapter, the stories are unique, as are the individuals. Life Memory Recall was used to assist the healing of a case of arthritis and a few common weight problems. As can be seen from the examples I have included, there is certainly no absolute formula that can be used on all these individuals to obtain desired results. Because of the differences in cause and uniqueness of each individual's life experiences, a technique was needed that allowed for these differences, yet had the capability to be used by anyone and everyone. This is where Life Memory Recall works the best. Its success rests in its focus on individual experience and adaptability to all situations. The similarity exists in the process of recovering what is needed from a moment in the past in order to change the present in a way that results in improvements in an individual's health, well being or state of mind and heart.

As we review the results, we need to ask what they "real-ly" mean. We can see that the results are real enough by the outcomes of people's experiences. Yet, we need to ask, "Have these people truly been healed? And if healing occurs, what other common sufferings might be helped through this process?

CHAPTER 5

▼

WHAT IS HEALING?

Healing is change. It is a movement from one state to another, specifically from ill health to health. This seems to be a very obvious statement, but for an understanding of the effects of Life Memory Recall, which in most cases results in improved states of health, it is important first to identify healing as a transition, and then to develop a definition of "health" itself.

In order to know what health is, we need to expand our understanding of what illness is. It is common to associate health with the absence of disease involving the physical systems of our bodies. These illnesses have names, as if they have an identity of their own, running the gamut of everything from the common cold to the most painful and debilitating disease types. In no way here do I wish to down play the significance of the physical types of disease in people's lives. Nor do I want to dismiss the enormous strength that is often required to overcome such states of illness. However, to express an expanded view of what health truly is, we need to include an expanded view of disease; one that encompasses not just our physical bodies, but our minds and emotions as well. It can also include our spirit, that driving force for connection, in whatever way we choose to define it. For our purposes, all aspects of a person must be considered when discussing health. To begin, we need to redefine the word disease so that we will know what the lack of disease means—*health*. From here on, when referring to a state requiring a desired healing change, I will use the word dis-ease. This will include any and all references to being in a state of less than optimal health, and any and all aspects of change, whether physical, psychological, behavioral, emotional or spiritual.

This desired change then occurs as a change in the mind/body connections that make up who we are. They cannot be separated within the healing process. If, for example, a person is experiencing the physical expression of a dis-ease by outward symptoms, they would also experience less obvious emotional and psychological aspects as well. I say less obvious only in regard to what is traditionally searched for in treatment and symptom relief.

While the relief of physical symptoms is the normal focus of treatment, it may be the emotional attachment to the symptoms which is the most difficult to overcome, especially if this aspect goes untreated. And in my experience based on many client conversations, when the experience is of physical discomfort, the emotional aspect is often overlooked. Treatment has become focused on the physical and may be less effective where non-physical symptoms occur simultaneously. For example, while it is routine to take a pill to alleviate the discomfort of a headache, that same pill will not be able to alleviate a broken heart. Fortunately, this traditional view of healing is changing to one that recognizes that healing must occur with consideration of all levels of the mind/body connection. One look at the increase in the use of alternative and complementary therapies today would show just how much the traditional view has been altered.

The mind/body connection is changing our perception of the healing process itself. It is now understood and accepted that when we create a change in any aspect of our being, we inadvertently affect every other aspect of the same being. Healing of the physical cannot exist in a vacuum. When a physical symptom is relieved, an emotional or behavioral change will occur as well. One will always affect the other, resulting in behavior changes that are the direct result of the alleviation of physical dis-ease. Anyone who has experienced the healing of an illness already knows this. They have experienced the unseen internal changes that take place when healing occurs. I have no doubt that we have all seen this occur in others or in ourselves. With the freedom from dis-ease comes the freedom to see life differently.

This is well illustrated in Carlos's story; a change occurred in the physiological expression of a problem that had plagued him for years. Having identified his problem as a symptom expressed in his body, its cessation was obvious. In his particular case, the healing results proved even more gratifying, since the existence of his problem had been well documented by current medical standards. Carlos not only had a problem requiring healing, but a history of failed attempts regardless of the method he used. Life Memory Recall provided Carlos with the method for creating a transition toward improved health and well-being. The end result included both physiological healing, as well as subtle emotional changes that were not as apparent.

Once open to the concept of releasing a past life trauma as he perceived it, he also gained movement on the physiological and emotional levels of his being. Although not initially obvious, his later discussions with me proved that his outlook had been changed and that his return to a vigorous state, with increased stamina, was caused by more than the cessation of a physiological illness. No longer preoccupied by stomach pain, Carlos was able to test his inner strengths and confidence. His new abilities in the martial arts, demonstrated for him that he had received benefits beyond the physical. He had moved his belief system toward an acceptance of the visions his mind had created, and he was empowered to know that whatever he created for himself would be useful, meaningful and could be applied to his daily life. He recognized that the impossible was not only possible, but, in his case, a matter of fact.

This is the essence of healing, the change I have repeatedly stated as an outcome of Life Memory Recall work. Behavioral or psychological and emotional changes occurred simultaneously with physical changes. While in Carlos' case, the emotional changes were subtle compared to the physical changes, this is not always the case. For many people it is the psychological and emotional changes that signify healing, especially when a physiological condition is not the primary focus. This is true in the following story of Daniel. His story relates to a problem I have encountered all too often as a practicing therapist: alcoholism.

One day I received a call from a noticeably worried father. His nervousness and desperation were obvious as he told me about his 20 year old son, Daniel, who had a drinking problem. Barely audible, he went on to say, "I am afraid that he is an alcoholic."

He asked a number of questions about my background, and when he was finally calm enough for me to ask a few questions. I asked him what made him think his son had a problem.

He responded, "He goes out drinking with his friends and 'loses it'."

"What do you mean he loses it?"

"First, I have to tell you that he is a nice kid. He is a very giving person, the kind of person who you would want as a friend. Aside from the fact that he is my son, he's the kind of person I would enjoy having as a friend, except when he is drinking. When he is drinking he is another person. He is not mean when drinking; he just can't stop drinking. Then he'll get rowdy and seems to get into trouble."

"What kind of trouble, if I may ask?" I inquired, to which I learned that Daniel had lost his driver's license several times and at present was enrolled in a special driver education course for people who were caught driving while intoxicated (DWI). Along with the legal problems and loss of license, there were a number of car accidents. Fortunately, so far, none of the drinking while driving accidents had been severe or life threatening. However, Daniel's father was terribly afraid that if Daniel persisted with his current behavior, he just might seriously injure or kill himself, as well as someone else. This, neither men could live with. I asked if Daniel would be willing to call me and come to see me.

"Yes, but I'll have to come too. I'll have to drive him since he lost his license again recently."

Prior to giving out the directions to my office I reiterated my desire to talk to Daniel, and asked his father if he were sure Daniel would be receptive.

Having been reassured about the kind of work I did, Daniel's father admitted, "It was Daniel's idea. He's the one that heard about you and asked if I would be willing to take him to see you. I'm the one that needed to check it out first."

We then set up an appointment. About two weeks later Daniel and his father showed up as scheduled. I asked Daniel's father to make himself comfortable in the waiting room and explained to him that I would be with Daniel about an hour and a half to two hours. He could join us after our private session was finished.

Daniel was exactly as his father had described him. He was personable and easy to talk with. He had no difficulty discussing his drinking and the troubles he's been in as a result. His openness about this problem would make Daniel a receptive subject for Life Memory Recall work. He was extremely accepting of the idea and even more willing to be rid of the drinking problem.

As the process of inducing a relaxed state begins and the client and I move ahead to discovering any past life memories, there are times when I can pursue whether there may be more than one. In Daniel's case we identified that there were two past memories, each contributing to his current problem.

In the first past life memory, he saw himself as a twenty-five year old female. She was quite attractive, tall, and elegant, appearing in a long dress with her hair pulled away from her face in a bun. Daniel sensed that she was wealthy, although particular details indicating this were not explored. Daniel saw her as she was walking down a cobble stone street on a gray day. The misty, overcast sky seemed to be everywhere. As he described it, not only did the general atmosphere look gray, but all the old stone buildings took on the same grayness. It was a grayness that carried with it feelings of dullness and sadness.

The woman entered what seemed to be a general store and was looking for something. She kept looking and looking. She found herself going up and down the aisles, almost frantic in her search for some particular item. As hard as she searched, she could not find what she was looking for, and finally locates a clerk to ask for the location of the item. At this point, Daniel's voice had an edge of desperation in it. The clerk directed the woman to the pharmacy. She had been searching for a medicine, a cough medicine. Eventually she found it.

What Daniel and I discovered is that she had no illness. She used the medicine as an excuse, to cover up her need to imbibe. She was an alcoholic. This is how she was able to have some alcohol, while feeling that she was hiding the fact from everyone else.

After Daniel and I learned this, we explored the life of this woman in greater detail in order to find the cause for her drinking, which in turn would later be related to Daniel's drinking. Finding the cause, we might then find the necessary release for Daniel's desired current life changes.

The more that we explored, the more that Daniel's first impression proved true. She did indeed appear wealthy, living in a large, beautiful home. Hired staff catered to her every need or whim. The inside of the house was wonderful, according to Daniel. The woodwork and trim was milled to perfection with numerous carved designs. Especially nice were the oversized windows that served as a frame to peer out at an immense, beautifully landscaped lawn. Noticing the windows, Daniel also noted how light and bright the inside of the house felt. All seemed light and bright except the woman. She had absolutely nothing to do, and he could feel her overwhelming boredom. She spent her days entertaining her lady friends and sipping her cough medicine. With friends, there would also be wine or cocktail-type drinks served. Her husband, a very busy man, was hardly ever home.

Even with all the physical trappings of comfort and splendor surrounding this woman, she could only feel loneliness and sadness. Her drinking served to diminish her ability to feel the hurt that had come from the loneliness. It compensated it, numbed it, until finally, it destroyed her. She died at a relatively early age from an overdose of the medicine, and perhaps other substances as well. According to the past life memory timeframe Daniel described, the cough medication most likely contained other potentially dangerous and/or addictive substances. It was unlikely that Daniel knew anything about the pharmacology of the time, yet his past life memory's conclusion was plausible.

I proceeded to assist Daniel in finding out whether this was a related cause by asking him whether the woman died to escape from the lonely life she perceived she had, or if it was just an accidental happening. Daniel was not sure, but was confident that this piece of the memory did not matter compared to the feelings of the need to drink. We worked together until Daniel could release this life of addiction.

Daniel's second past life memory would prove to play an equally important role in transforming his problem. Alcohol again played a major role. However, this experience was a positive one. Daniel saw himself as a male in his twenties, living in the United States. The time period was somewhere in the late 1800's. He was a wood worker and a furniture builder, someone who truly had a passion for his craft. Daniel first saw himself carefully and lovingly "shaving" a fine piece of furniture. Daniel described clearly that he was feeling that he was doing what gave him pleasure and he had a good sense of esteem in this life. He was married and had several children. I heard pride ringing in Daniel's voice as he said, "I was a good husband and father."

The exploration of this past life memory quickly made it clear that Daniel was proud of being who he was and what he stood for. Once the circumstances were clearly established, I asked Daniel to go to the time in this former life that was affecting Daniel today. He moved to a time when he was thirty-five. He was dressed in what he said was his only suit. He saw himself standing with members of his family next to him, his wife and two children. All were dressed in their best. Daniel described how he appeared. He saw himself standing proud, although he looked sad. Everyone was looking in the same direction. Before long, I discovered that they were at a funeral, the funeral for the man's father. His father was an alcoholic, as Daniel said, "a drunk." Daniel described him as a father who did not properly care for his family, a father who spent his money on liquor instead of taking care of his family. It was the difference between this father and the son in the past life that Daniel noticed most. Whereas the father created disappointment, Daniel, seeing himself as the man, felt only pride. He had done what his father had not been able to do. His father's alcoholism drove the son to be a better man. In spite of alcohol and as a result of alcoholism, the cabinetmaker son had a fulfilled life, dying in his seventies, full of contentment.

It was this part of the past life memory that Daniel could take back with him. Instead of releasing a negative experience, he was able to maintain a positive one.[1] Daniel, through the Life Memory Recall process, was able to accept the feeling of being a good family man and a nondrinker. He accepted that life could be as fulfilling, if not more so, without alcohol. Once accepted, a wonderfully calming effect became obvious in Daniel. It showed on his face, which no longer held the stress it had at the beginning of our session. The muscles in Daniel's body also relaxed. A smile crossed Daniel's face and the session came to an end.

For Daniel, he was able to rid himself of a past life memory of a drinking problem that had plagued him, while also keeping the marvelous feeling of what it was like to have had a life that was happy and sober.

When Daniel returned for a follow-up session, he told me that since leaving my office he no longer had the urge for drinking the volume of alcohol he had before. He even tested this by going out for a few beers with friends. For the first time since he could remember, he had a couple then stopped. He expressed how wonderful it was to go out, be able to enjoy himself and have no desire to continue drinking until he found himself in a stupor.[2]

To Daniel and his father, his behavior was a dramatic change that affected other aspects of his being. With the physical desires removed,

---

1. Life Memory Recall allows for both the release and retention of life memory experience, depending on which is required to positively affect the current life circumstance.

2. I made no personal or professional comments on Daniel's having a beer or two with regard to appropriate or inappropriate behavior, given his previous difficulty in alcohol management. I was pleased to hear, however, that he felt his problem was now manageable and this change was the healing he wanted. For some clients with addictive behaviors, the Life Memory Recall process goes further and allows them to completely leave behind their previous problem, providing them with the strength they need to make the necessary lifestyle changes this would require. The technique creates the opportunity for healing, the rest is a matter of individual choice.

Daniel's psychological, emotional and even spiritual self improved. Change occurred and therefore, as we've defined it, healing occurred.

With Life Memory Recall, change and healing occur on many levels. The technique creates a process of transformation from a state of dis-ease toward increased health, often including a deeper sense of well-being. The levels of change that result from this technique can range from the mundane to the miraculous, as the stories presented herein will attest. Each true story will demonstrate an aspect of a healing transformation and the limitlessness of healing possibilities as defined by the unique experiences encountered by individuals no different than yourselves. The individuals' need for healing is as unique as their personal characters, and the dis-ease process each experiences is dissimilar, yet, they encounter a similar connection simply by the choice they made along a path for recovery. For them, the pathway led to a rediscovery of past life experiences which, when allowed to integrate with their current life situations, released them from any angst they may have associated to these past life experiences. The common factor was that a change in perception preceded the healing transformations that followed. This we've witnessed in the preceding chapters as well as in this one. Their "life stories" were as particular to them as yours is to you. The difference is that they have already recovered them and have successfully integrated them into their healing process. The good news is that the same understanding, methods, and experiences are available to anyone through the Life Memory Recall process, regardless of what unique circumstances a person faces.

Departing from Daniel's problem with alcohol, other experiences of healing are presented throughout this book to further delve into the process of healing and the personal stories accompanying it. I will be exploring the deeper meaning within the transformational process (moving toward health and healing) in order to allow a greater understanding of past life rediscovery and its impact for life recovery. Life Memory Recall therapy will be better defined, as I have experienced it, through actual case histories. And I will introduce the concept of Guided Light Therapy, a technique new to the general understanding of hypnotherapy based on my work with my colleague, Hollie. It represents a method that was created by the need to integrate the past life (regression) experience beyond its customary framework. Moving beyond the discovery and incorporation of past life memories, Life Memory Recall and Guided Light Therapy both include every moment up to the present and even beyond. These methods are expanded to include all experiences that make a person who they are, at any given point in time. This is another example of how these therapies have transcended limitations and the definition of healing possibilities.

Thus far, we have demonstrated that the physical transformation from disease to well-being by utilizing past life recall can be profoundly evident. Equally evident is that healing in its subtler forms, which are just as significant, also happen through this rediscovery/recovery work. By subtler forms, we simply mean forms less apparent on the outside, such as emotional, behavioral and/or psychological symptom resolution. Subtler and less evident than these are the spiritual transformations that often occur. By spiritual, we mean a sense of connection within ourselves to something greater than ourselves. Although not readily apparent from the outside, it is often the spiritual transformation that has the greatest life impact. It can often involve a life style change as part of the healing process, as was seen in Daniel's story above.

As I noted at the beginning of this chapter, healing is a transformational process. In any form, it represents change. By sharing the stories and experiences in this book I strive to express to the reader their own potential for healing. While this pathway may not be for everyone, it is certainly accessible to anyone. It should be undertaken with diligence and an awareness of its potential effects. *Healing in any form is profound!*

While the experience of immediate physical change can be exhilarating beyond expectation, other changes may be less obvious and may not be as immediately experienced. For this reason, it is most essential that the person undergoing therapy be open and willing to allow healing to manifest as it will. There is always a *positive* change, whether it is physical, psychological or spiritual, though it may not happen immediately, or in the manner expected. Often physical healing will occur after some time has passed, with or without traditional medical intervention, once other aspects of the healing process have taken place. In many cases, a change in general outlook is encountered first. By changing the outlook, the relationship between oneself and their disease process or problem is inextricably and positively altered, opening the way to further healing.

Through this process, instead of the dis-ease controlling us, we enter a state of mind that allows us to take charge of the situation. We are now able to more effectively approach a solution. Should further intervention be required to eradicate the symptoms at hand, we are ready with confidence to develop a working plan of attack.

As we consider what healing is, it is necessary to include the idea of well-being. We need to address change on each and every level of possibility, because for many common problems or illnesses a too narrow definition of healing may impede positive change, especially when a problem expresses itself less in a physical way than in an emotional, behavioral or psychological way. Life Memory Recall allows each facet of oneself its expression and therefore, directly affects one's sense of "well"—being also.

As limiting thoughts are replaced with the calm of greater inner strength and new possibility, a person can approach the illness or problem they have with a mindset that has the ability to let go, to look beyond the current experience and realize that the future has yet to be determined and therefore is changeable.

How does one get to this point? By accessing the pictures of past experiences and integrating them into useful and empowering information relative to the present. The person creates the structure from which to glean insights regarding their association with any current restraints inadvertently placed on the process of healing. For example, this person may not even realize what s/he needs to heal prior to it being revealed in the recovered "life stories." There may be aspects that s/he was not considering, such as the need to emotionally heal while searching for physical healing. A person's spiritual connection of unlimited potential may be veiled from view and require a re-familiarization with their internal dialogue in order to access a belief of continued hope.

The past life experience may assist in revealing patterns of psychological imprisonment that deters a sense and expression of self-empowerment. Whatever the need, this therapy can allow an effective transition from a point of non-knowing to a greater awareness of understanding and integration along the pathway of healing.

The true stories in the following chapters will also serve as a guide to the many levels of healing associated with the transformational process many find with Life Memory Recall and Guided Light Therapy. They are the examples to show that this therapy assists in healing whatever is required in order to overcome the obstacles at hand. As different as the experiences are in each case you will read about, there exists one extraordinary detail of commonality, a mutual thread that binds all these unique individuals together. This thread is the therapy's most marvelous feature! It *always* works at some level to effect change—the process of healing transformation, and it works because it is always accompanied by a personal revelation. Simply, it reveals the uniqueness of individual life stories, past and present. Even more, it helps to create the pictures of the future. Together, this therapy offers help and support without hindering any other efforts underway in the search for healing. A person never has to be concerned about "negative side-effects" with other therapies underway. It is, in fact, a wonderful addition to any healing regimen and path already taken. The advantage is in what it additionally reveals about the healing pathways and one's relationship to it that otherwise would not be revealed.

In order to understand the therapy's use as it applies to the development of a personal and revelatory relationship, we must define the process more succinctly. All revelation involves a personal desire for change. The recognition of this desire is the first realization that occurs when considering additional treatment therapies beyond those recognized, accepted or promoted in the treatment of any state of ill health. These therapies apply to individuals who seek a healing outcome greater than what they are currently experiencing. There are many effective modalities of treatment available that either reduce the symptoms of a disease state or provide a cure. Yet, not everyone encounters the same profound effects. For the individuals less satisfied with the results of any chosen treatment, the therapy we suggest should be viewed as an opportunity; a safe and comfortable adjunct to care already given. It affords one a wonderful additional option in a quest for complete healing. And it opens the door to a connection between the body, mind and heart.

This type of healing is healing of not just the problem and process but includes the complete healing of the self. It incorporates the holistic view of treatment currently popularized in today's paradigm of healing. It moves away from the desire of the cessation of symptoms only and into the need for understanding the healing process fully. The desire is for a true cure not symptom relief. The desire is the cessation of the Expression of any dis-ease or illness while finding a life of greater well being in the process.

This is the nature of healing when it incorporates all aspects that make us human. This is the personal revelation that is revealed through past life experiences when integrated into the current life circumstances. And this is what we offer in the telling of the events and experiences of the many people who have openly searched for the additional help needed in developing a transformation for themselves.

As mentioned earlier, healing begins with the desire for change. It is only necessary at the beginning to recognize that a deep connection of need exists that propels the search for each and every opportunity available that may offer the desired change. Once established, the pathways toward the opportunity for transformation are automatically initiated. From this point on, a common internal motivation takes hold that can be expressed as a sequence of personal understandings that are the underpinnings behind all rediscovery and recovery work we have encountered thus far. They are the mechanism by which transformation proceeds in expected and predictable ways. They are also the indicators for future success.

The first understanding of the healing process beyond the primary need to heal or create change, is the **willingness** to heal. The second understanding and of equal importance, is the **acceptance** that change *can* occur. Willingness must be addressed first. Once it has been established, acceptance can enter. And at this point we begin the healing process. A working template for healing to take place has now been created. Acceptance involves a holistic view. What this means is simply that no aspect of the self is overlooked in the healing process. What we think, feel, sense, and experience must be considered collectively and as a whole. The person we are at each and every moment is considered along side the illness or problem. In this way, we are not limited in the depth of change that is possible. We are no longer defined by the disease process but are removed from a narrow view of thinking and are free to participate in our own healing process from an expanded realm of possibilities. Therefore, acceptance first begins by being receptive to all that we are regardless of the current expression of an illness or problem. Then it moves us to accepting the illness or problem as a current state of being which you are willing to change. This is the time when Life Memory Recall and Guided Light Therapy enters the healing process, regardless of the kinds of healing that are required.

We can easily see how each individual obtains the desired healing by relating the results they received to the past life experience. What may be less obvious are the essential links between the memories recalled. They are the links that tie the memories to the healing process. In each example, a willingness for change initiated the process. Each individual that came for help was ready to receive it. Their willingness for change allowed them to accept the experience, whatever it may have been. In willingness, we learn to open ourselves to new possibilities. Preconceived notions are left behind and attention is focused on the work itself. In so doing, judgment and expectation are left behind. Instead, hope for change replaces them. Freedom from judgment and expectation allows acceptance to flow more easily. The acceptance allows the experience to unfold such that a story can be told.

In a regressed state then, the experience of past life memory occurs. It is allowed to randomly flow without a conscious effort to justify or categorize it. During the process, it is not necessary to judge whether the experience is real or fictional. Instead, it is just allowing the experience to unfold. A person remains present in the experience itself, most often enjoying the memory as each image or feeling is created or sensed. Although you are consciously aware of what is happening, it is the willingness to let go of the normal judgments that allows the healing process to continue until a root cause, the driver, is found. This was and is the process followed in the previous examples and those yet to come.

The acceptance of the experience comes next, immediately or in time. I have, with a greater understanding from the many years of doing this work, seen over and over how important this step is to the healing process. When I talk about acceptance, I don't mean that the life memory must be accepted as real. I mean that it has simply to be accepted as an experience that has caused a change to occur, and for this change to be accepted as a process of healing. Once the past life memory has been found, there can be nothing less than change in one form or another. It is no different than changing a moment of your past. If a person could do this, the person would not be the same. Many times I've heard people express that if they could have done this or that differently then his or her life would be different. They are right in this. However, while it is impossible to actually redo our previous moments, it is possible to actually *relive* our previous moments and do something different. We can re-experience our moments, whether in this life or by a recalled past memory. It is the beauty of this work, for only in this way, can we go back and "do" things differently. We still can't change what has occurred within our consciousness, but we can find a deeper and truer meaning that may have been previously obscured and it is this that creates the needed and desired change.

In a past life memory, we can find the same or related situations in our current life and "re-do" them by the "seeing" a life that has similar meaning. The events related to today's problems are literally given new forms from which the meaning can become clear. If someone is plagued by an eating disorder, as in the previous chapter, a past life memory can be discovered that is related to either a lack or excess of food in a past life memory. Its relation to the current problem can then be understood and released, let go of. In this way, the person afflicted can "re-do" the current problem through this releasing of the past life memory. By saying, in a sense, no more of this in the past memory, they are saying no more in the current situation. It is that simple. A change occurs as a result, and this change is healing.

This is the general mechanism for creating change through the Life Memory Recall and Guided Light Therapy process. Within the willingness to accept any and all experiences that release past events associated in our minds with our current problem, the healing process begins. The results can be seen in the transition from an ill or problematic state to one of better health or well-being. Each person has an equal ability to access this inner knowledge. Through the use of past life discovery/recovery, an option is created which can assist in finding the hidden answers. This is especially effective when options for healing have become limited, when medication or traditional therapy alone has not provided the results someone is searching for. It is especially useful when traditional avenues no longer have anything to offer.

What is even more exciting is that this option can be added to any ongoing therapy, working synergistically, not in contradiction. It never interferes with any other choices made or treatment rendered. It can also assist a person by healing aspects of an illness or problem that medicine alone cannot provide. Often, physical and/or psychological symptoms can be relieved or reduced by medication, but it is rare if not impossible for these medications to heal the emotional or spiritual symptoms without further intervention. For those individuals experiencing these aspects of illness or problems, this therapy adds to the healing process in these areas. This is essential to be able to move past temporary relief to a true cure.

Today, it has become well known that a human being is made up of many components. We are not just a biological system run by a grouping of nerves in the brain. We are much more. Our psychological, emotional and spiritual self must be included in order to enter into a healing journey that will allow profound change. Since Life Memory Recall and Guided Light Therapy automatically involve the physical, psychological, emotional, and spiritual components within its healing process, it has the capability of creating changes on extraordinary levels.

Just as extraordinary as the potential results are, so too was the evolution of the therapy processes themselves. Guided by the results, later conversations with Hollie, and always looking for the experiences that created the greatest amount of change, the new processes emerged. From an understanding of past life regression therapy, came Life Memory Recall. When the definition of Past Life Regression and its process expanded and changed, so too did the capabilities of what this work could provide in regard to healing effects.

What I had yet to realize was that there was more to come than just a change in definition. In setting my intention to find a way to serve as both a therapist and healing agent for my clients, a second adjustment in my own beliefs about this work took place. This final adjustment began the day I welcomed Hollie, a new client, into my office.

Hollie's arrival marked the beginning of the evolution of Life Memory Recall and concluded with the development of the technique called Guided Light Therapy. As you will see as you read on, it was this therapy as a component of the Life Memory Recall process that created the avenue for me to bring you the stories of healing in this book. It is a concept that transformed everything, including me. In this transformation was created the ability to cause even more significant change in people's lives. And as I said at the beginning of this chapter, change is the answer to the question, "What is healing?"

CHAPTER 6

▼

HOLLIE'S STORY

To my surprise, August 3, 1999 turned out to be a life-changing day. It began as most days do, with the usual morning rituals of waking a child, preparing breakfast, packing a lunch and lovingly seeing my daughter and husband off for the day. I was growing used to staying behind, since a workplace situation had left me unemployed just a month before. Having decided that this unexpected turn of events represented an opportunity to assess a changing future, it was agreed that I would take some time "off" before re-entering the workforce; an agreement that I welcomed.

The previous year had been one of extraordinary time commitments and demands on my energy. I held an executive position in a large corporation, which was undergoing major reorganization brought about by a merger and downsizing. The bottom line was changing, as was the fundamental character of the company. It was the perfect picture of corporate America in the '90s; loyalty and camaraderie was being replaced by fear and self-protection. While the financial picture for the company improved, the individual risk of unemployment increased. Everyone was flexed and stretched to new limits, and many people were shown the door. I was no exception.

Prior to leaving the company, I was in the middle of adjusting to the changes at work while also pursuing a Master's degree in Management. My weekly schedule was a tangled mess, nothing a sane person might design. But, thanks to the help of an understanding husband, I made it to graduation day. Two weeks later, I was dryly told that my efforts at the company were no longer necessary. They had simply decided that my tasks had been completed to such a degree that they could be self-managed for quite some time. I had done a great job and therefore, was no longer required to monitor the progress. Instead, I was offered what I considered a distasteful alternative if I continued my employment or a severance package if I left. I was fortunate, at least I had been given the opportunity to gracefully exit.

As I got into my car for the hour drive home I was filled with emotion. But it wasn't what you might expect. I began to laugh! An overwhelming feeling of freedom began to surge through me. I had been so ready for a break, but was too afraid to take the steps myself. I had put so much of myself on hold to accomplish what had been asked of me, and I felt a great relief that things had changed so that I no longer had to.

Then it hit me. I represented a huge potential lost for the company. If I had stayed I would have been a resource that would have willingly sacrificed as needed, done whatever they had asked. The company could have expanded my role and I would have attacked it with the same fervor as before. I would have given up personal satisfaction for meeting company objectives. I would have become a true corporate identity and ladder climber. I was amazed at the realization. I was shocked at the thought that I would have held my personal life and those I cared about as second in my life.

Then I asked myself "What the hell have you been doing and how did you get here?" This is when the laughter rolled out of my chest and into my throat before I had a chance to question it. What a fool I'd been, giving so much of myself to a company that didn't even care about me, about anyone! It struck me then as extremely funny, almost ludicrous. Later, of course, I would deal with a host of other less pleasant, sometimes frightening emotions as I began to question, "Who am I?" and "Now what?"

So began my search for the answers to these questions, a search that led down many paths and to many places, one of which was the office of Dr. Norton Berkowitz. For more than 10 years, I had pursued an interest in so-called New Age concepts and alternative and complementary medicine by attending lectures and participating in numerous seminars and workshops. Prior to entering the corporate world, I had practiced as a general dentist for many years. During this time my patients continually challenged my knowledge, sometimes about dentistry and often on other subjects. When we weren't discussing a particular filling material or the latest dental techniques, the conversation became more personal in nature.

Patients began to share their own experiences with me, and in ever increasing numbers they began to mention things they were "trying". These "things" turned out to be experiments in new ways of understanding themselves and the world around them. Alternative ways of thinking about relationships, abilities, new insights found, methods of healing, and many, many more subjects were brought to my attention via the dental office. I listened and learned from them all. And as different patients began to report similar experiences, I took note. I began to read. I soon wanted to experience some of it, too.

One day I finally acted upon my feelings and participated in my first workshop. There I learned about touch therapy, a technique wherein an individual could set his/her thoughts in such a way that through physical touch, comfort could be provided to another. Pretty good, I thought, considering nine out of ten people entering my office could benefit by being comforted in some way. Rarely did I meet anyone who actually enjoyed the dental experience! Fear and anxiety were the most common denominators among patients receiving dental care. Maybe, I thought, this would be something I could use.

That first workshop was all it took to get me started on a path of searching for whatever new and wonderful things were out there, things I had, as yet, heard nothing about. My first motivation was to learn ways to make my patients more comfortable with any procedure they needed. This primarily involved methods that helped to manage or alleviate the perceived stress of a dental visit. Interestingly, the more I found out about the various methods, the more I discovered I needed to know. I was gaining an appetite for researching any and all concepts new to my understanding of "how everything works". Each new find led me toward a better understanding of what and how people wanted change. Later, I recognized that I was changing in the process; that the questing path I started was as much for me as for anyone else. I fully enjoyed learning and sharing ideas, concepts and beliefs. I also enjoyed sharing the various methods of help I found, even those that at first seemed as strange as anything possibly could be.

Eventually, as I worked with the newly acquired information, a realization took hold that maybe some of the so-called strange methods were REAL. Maybe there really was more to human help than the eye can see. Maybe I have a potential to help myself and others in ways that remain untapped until the mind is ready to let go and become accepting of things, regardless of how strange they first seem. Whatever the case, as I incorporated some of the new concepts into daily practice, things around me changed. I continued to change, too. When I used a method or technique for whatever purpose it was designed for, repeatable outcomes occurred. It became hard to automatically shut out any ideas that all this "stuff" was a bit weird or kind of crazy. There were many workshops and lessons that appeared ridiculous to me at first. Yet, if I was brave enough to remain open-minded, I always learned something that eventually proved tangible and useful. Not all of the learning was to my liking, nor were all of the lessons highly fruitful. However, each had something important to say about my need to cast aside my judgments before I tried them. It was this understanding that allowed me to visit Norton Berkowitz.

I had decided, following my departure from corporate life, to take some time to truly evaluate where I was and who I was. I wanted to pursue a deeper understanding of myself and the last ten years of knowledge seeking. I wanted to find out how to reprioritize what was really important in my life and clean out any thinking that had contributed to my veering off course. Silently, I had decided that the summer and early fall would be a time of great experimentation. I committed three months to myself to explore prior to re-entering the workforce. For once, I was just going to search for answers as the wind sounded them.

The wind brought me Norton Berkowitz, literally! Within a matter of eight days his name was spoken to me three times by different people as someone I might want to meet. I was told that he was a hypnotherapist, mainstream and alternative, and always a professional. My path, up to this point, taught me that when I hear or feel or say something repeatedly, I should pay attention. So, having incorporated this as part of my truth, I asked myself, "How often would a name like Berkowitz come up anyway?"

Knowing the answer, I called him and had a brief discussion over the phone about his therapy. Norton asked me what I wanted to work on after he had explained the past life regression process in limited detail. Since I hadn't really thought much further than to make the call, my answer was a bit vague. I quickly searched my mind, and as I did so I rambled on about the recent changes in my life and the transition period I was working through. I briefly mentioned that I was exploring, with great curiosity, what makes me tick, and primarily was looking for answers to who I was and how I got to the present moment. He had been mentioned to me because of his work in past life regression and I had an interest in seeing if any of this applied to me or my current state. He was congenial about my lack of intention regarding my needs and with little more said we made an appointment. As yet, August third was just another day, and once penned into my calendar, I didn't give it a second thought.

Only later when I looked at my calendar, did I even remember I had made an appointment. I had been trying to live each day as it came rather than be guided by schedules. Here it was August third, and there was my appointment with Norton. So, directions in hand, I headed for his office. I was expecting no more than the chance to satisfy my curiosity about his work, maybe investigate yet another method of help. After all, I thought, he had been highly recommended many times by people who said they had gained wonderful insights from working with him. I thought maybe I could gain some too. And if nothing else, it would be fun to do.

I arrived on schedule and he greeted me at his front door. I was, to be honest, more intrigued by the extraordinary stained glass which hung behind the door's window, than beginning our work for the day. I entered and we exchanged a few pleasantries as he guided me to his office. It felt wonderfully inviting and comfortable. A couch would serve as my seat for the next hour or so. His seat was a well-worn chair.

We sat across from one another to begin the process. This was also comfortable. Instead of facing each other while staring at a blank wall behind him, I was looking out a wall of windows. The quality of the light and the beauty of the trees outside provided relief from the usual tenseness of meeting in a traditional doctor's office. Norton's manner was also disarming. His speech was calm and gentle in tone. He seemed genuinely pleased to meet me. At this point, I really had nothing to say, so I was relieved when he began the conversation. In just a few moments, he was telling me about himself and his work and I found myself volunteering an equal exchange. Surprisingly, I found I had quite a bit to say about myself.

We talked a bit about my recent life changes. I mentioned that maybe we could find some new information that would be useful. I was interested in finding new possibilities for myself by getting to know myself in different ways; that maybe, past life work held some new meaning for me. Either way, I approached the whole idea with enthusiasm and increasing curiosity.

Following a bit more discussion, we developed a short list of possible pieces of information to retrieve. One of those pieces was to see if I could explore a near death experience that occurred when I was about 16 months old. The incident had been barely mentioned by my family other than the fact of it, so I didn't know too much about it. And, until now, it had never occurred to me to ask. I figured it was part of my past and that was that. I was not aware of any major side effects, at least that I knew of, that made me think any other way. Now, however, I saw an opportunity to question whether or not I could go back and remember the incident. I felt no fear as I approached this because I felt I would just be imagining the whole thing anyway. Besides, I had already on occasion during various meditation exercises, tried to go back and couldn't. So I really expected very little from the experience. Later, I would learn just how important it was that I was relaxed about the concept, free to explore the possibility without anticipation or preconceived expectation.

Norton was in the process of explaining the hypnotherapy technique for inducing a regressed state when I refocused on what he was saying.

"I'll first take you to a past experience that you'll view as entirely pleasurable. Then, once we know you can get to where you want, we'll explore some of the items we discussed. Are you ready to get started? Do you have any more questions before we begin?"

"No, I think I'm ready. Do you mind if I lie down? I find it easier to fully relax and meditate this way and I think I'll be more comfortable."

"Make yourself as comfortable as you'd like. I'll be starting the tape now. Let's begin."[1]

At first I was fully aware of everything Norton was saying. He began a sequence of suggestions that helped to create a visual image within my thoughts, like watching a movie, which after a short time became more vivid. I had gone from thinking about what Norton had asked me to picture, to feeling what I was picturing. Instead of watching the movie, I felt like I was in the movie. This was quite relaxing and freeing, like exploring a new adventure. The setting of my movie was warm and soothing, the sun shone brightly. I was in a self-created paradise. I became less and less aware of my body lying on Norton's couch, and more and more aware of this dream-body, experiencing wonderment over the serene and beautiful setting I had created. I was actively participating in everything as if it were real.

I walked along a beautiful path of gray stone. To one side was a small river; to the other was foliage of a green I can only describe as vibrantly alive. Deep in the background I heard Norton's voice moving me forward, clear yet distant. I willingly moved as it suggested, envisioning myself getting ready to cross a bridge of my own making. The bridge my mind created was short and made of conspicuously placed stone, arching gradually over a shallow and meandering stream. The voice asked me to cross over to

---

1. Norton always audio-tapes the sessions; for his notes review later and to provide a session copy to each client. Personally, having the session taped help me to feel more relaxed about him and what was going to happen.

its far side whenever I felt ready to do so. Had I not heard these words, I would have enjoyed just staying in the beauty I had created around me. Yet, intrigued by what might be on the other side, I was propelled across.

When I reached the other side I begin to describe out loud what I saw. I was able to describe not only the environment around me, but a person who appeared there as well. I followed this person while remaining a bit in the background, completely unnoticed and unobtrusive. This person appeared to be a peddler. He carried his "wares" on his back tied by a line that was slung over his shoulder. His wares were rough hammered pots and pans. Somehow, I was able to actually feel what the peddler was feeling inside, even though I stood back in the distance. He made a meager living by selling from town to town. He was alone and enjoyed his solitary freedom. A quiet man from the outside, inside he was a virtual sponge, actively learning and taking in everything around him. I somehow knew that he was fully aware and appreciative of each circumstance he experienced that life had to offer. Nothing was forgotten. In this way, he brought not only his pots and pans to each small town, but a connection to the larger world, bringing news and personal tidbits of information to the curious townsfolk.

This scene continued until Norton's gentle, persuading voice asked that I move forward in this life to a time that has a purpose for me. *Zoom*. I instantly saw the same man. However, he had aged. Guessing he was in his last years, I still recognized him immediately. He was no longer surrounded by the clank of his pots and pans. Instead, he was sitting beside a mud hut on a well-placed rock with children surrounding him. I realized as I stepped forward to get a closer look, that I was viewing him through the eyes of a young child, and that they were my eyes. As the scene changed, so had I. I could feel what it felt like to be in the body of a three-year old. There were no concerns in this young mind. There was only the focus on this talking stranger. Curiosity was the prevailing emotion. There was such a present joy in just watching, it was as if nothing else mattered but the moment. This child was smiling, free of any miscellaneous or distracting thoughts. There were no worries or concerns about needing to be anywhere else.

Strangely, I could feel what it meant to be this child while still feeling and sensing everything else in full awareness. It quickly crossed my mind how foreign and forgotten this childhood freedom had become in my adult life. I recognized that I was rarely free to just be, always thinking that something should be getting done or that there was someplace else I needed to be. Remembering how to be free in these brief moments was a gift I could have savored for quite some time.

Breaking the momentary lapse in vision, beckoned by Norton's ever-present guidance, I was asked to move closer and relay to him what I was experiencing. I did, turning my attention back to the events I created, telling him that the man had become a storyteller. He was weaving a marvelous tale about a teacher of the people he once saw. He was saying how many would come to hear his words whenever he spoke. I found a place among the other children to sit and listen. I was again filled with wonderment and pure pleasure. The enjoyment of this moment filled me entirely.

Interrupted by the soft directions from Norton to take this feeling and come back with it to our starting place, the scene immediately vaporized. I was instantly aware that it was gone and I was standing where this experience had begun. I was again on my stony gray path on the opposite side of the bridge. Asked to now move to another point in time, I complied and, coaxed by Norton, entered my own life at sixteen months of age. Out of a seeming void, I slowly became aware of a different setting as if I was waking up in a new room. This time I did not cross the bridge, the scene just seemed to appear as a pinpoint that opened up into full view.

I begin to describe it in detail. It was a kitchen. The table was a molded, metal-framed monster with a gray, marbled-looking top. A stove of equal proportion jutted from a near wall. It too, stood like a metal monster with huge round knobs. A refrigerator, appearing dwarfed by the table and stove, was facing the stove against the adjacent wall. This room seemed small compared to what was in it. As I continued to gaze about, I saw a woman standing by a white porcelain sink. It was my mother. Her hands were buried in a sink, moving dishes from a frothy bath to a countertop. I felt no need to engage her, but accepted her presence and activity as simple fact. I was feeling completely satisfied and something about this scene felt very ordinary. Its clarity was astounding.

I then focused my awareness back to myself. I felt as if I were peering out at this kitchen from a body that was my own, but not my own. I was astonished when I saw small arms and pudgy legs jutting outward. They felt entirely attached to me. I couldn't see the body they were connected to. I didn't have to. It felt like mine. It was mine. It was then that I realized I was seated. I liked this because I was seated at a point that felt very high, and it was this seat that allowed me to look about the room. My toes were wiggling and my arms flaying. I was having a very good time.

As I watched my appendages, I could clearly see I was in an old wooden highchair. Even though I couldn't see its straight wooden back, I knew there was a faded bunny painting just behind my shoulder blades. There was also a tray in front. On this tray was an assortment of plastic dishes. They were placed and removed from this tray by another child who was seated lower than me. I recognized her as my older sister as a three and a half-year old. She was playing with me by setting up this little wooden shelf with these plastic pieces. I would gladly grab them, bang them a few times and toss them over the wooden tray. To me, they just disappeared into a place unknown, a void below. Each time the pieces were tossed out, my sister would magically produce them again causing sheer delight inside of me. Returning them started the process of banging and dropping all over again.

I could feel that I was smiling. My sister also gave me a spoon to bang, or so I thought, not knowing any other purpose for it than to make noise. Actually, she repeatedly motioned with her own spoon a dipping action into these empty plastic "pieces" or bowls. Each time she replaced a thrown bowl, she tried to get me to do the same dipping action, sometimes holding my fingers around the spoon. I preferred the banging. Repeatedly she gave me the spoon and repeatedly I returned it to the void until one time when there was something on it, a syrupy pink substance. It found its way to my mouth with my sister's coaxing and it tasted sweet. I looked and saw more of this "pink stuff" in one of the bowls. She began to feed it to me, grasping my little hand as before, and I welcomed it. I stopped throwing everything off the tray in exchange for receiving this goodie. She was smiling, and seemed pleased to be playing this new game.

This was the last image I recalled as I felt a change happening inside of me. The feeling was as if I was somehow moving away from her. I felt as though I was leaving this little body, going deeper inward yet feeling an increasing distance between us. The entire scene began to disperse from its edges, closing in, becoming an ever-smaller visual circle until finally it was gone. The scene went black.

Norton, never a step far behind, continued to ask me to relate what I was "seeing", which I did. But I also told him what I was feeling. Far from a still or motionless black void, I was clearly moving. Finally, out of the darkness, I was being propelled through a colorful tube, which swirled and circled about. It appeared as a rainbow of color, intertwined and streaming back and forth. It had a thickness and layered look to it. This tube spun around me while I was moving in a straight line forward. There was no fear or caution or any other emotion. I was simply moving. That was all I knew.

I was no longer feeling childlike. It was as if I was no particular age at all. I felt conscious and aware, yet had no sense of even having a body. In this awareness I began to notice the sensations this tube brought to me. While it swirled around me, it seemed as though time was passing by. I didn't see anything in particular, but felt sure that within the bands of color and waves of motion were the images of events passed. It felt as though I was experiencing what it would be like if the pictures of human history had been directly downloaded into my brain, much like the loading of software on a computer, never seeing the actual input but being able to access the results. To say that this sensation was odd would be a vast understatement. It was extraordinary. It was indescribable. The experience was beyond my understanding, yet, easily within my acceptance.

I tried to relay to Norton the sensation and vision I was experiencing, as he had asked. I simply said that time seemed to be passing me or I was moving through it. I couldn't tell which. I was however, without a doubt, heading in a forward direction with a sense of purpose.

Then, my journey through the tube came to an end. I began to speak about what had happened and what was currently unfolding. I found myself standing in what I will describe as an intensity of radiating light. The colors were gone and there was only a bright, white light. It had appeared like the beacon of a lighthouse that began like a pinpoint in the center of the colored tube. It grew in size until that is all there was. Norton asked me how I felt, and asked some general questions. Since there appeared to be nothing but this light, there was very little to say after this point. Therefore, he suggested I remember this place and the extraordinary peacefulness I had told him I felt while there and return to the present moment.

Having heard Norton's directions, I planned to return as I had in the experience before this one. The scene had begun to fade and I could feel myself returning to our predetermined starting point. However, I suddenly felt something very different. Instead of easily finding my way, I felt a giant pull in the opposite direction. I was feeling compelled to stay in this lit up place. Each attempt at moving away from there only increased my need and desire to return. Finally, I stated to Norton that I needed to go back, be back in the light place, for some reason. Having had years of experience with this process, Norton had the wisdom to agree. So I returned.

My first words were, "There's someone here who wants to speak with us."

"What?" was Norton's instant reply, "Hollie, could you repeat that?"

"There's someone here who wants to speak to us."

What followed would be an event that changed the course of both of our lives. It was this one sentence, the outcome of Norton's and my first session, that resulted in bringing us together, although neither of us would know this until much later.

Fortunately, Norton's experience had also taught him to not disregard anything that happens during a Life Memory Recall session. He knew that all information was important regardless of how it was retrieved. Whoever that "someone" turned out to be, it was a way to get information that was useful to me. Norton pushed his own amazement and curiosity aside as he continued to ask questions about the encounter for my benefit. The more questions he asked, the more fascinating the responses became. Norton's intention at this time, was to provide a line of questioning that allowed for the near death experience I had described prior to the beginning of the session, meaningful content. He attempted to draw out information that could answer my questions of purpose as I was pursuing them in my present life.

What we received was far from expected. Instead of my responding directly to Norton's questions, it was that "someone" else who began to ask the questions and provide information, although I was not aware of this change in our dynamic at the time. As the session continued, a story was revealed that challenged both Norton's and my belief systems, and left us both stymied. The encounter and the information received left our imaginations reeling. It was as if Norton and I were students and the responses were meant specifically for us, to teach us. The things said were about our hearts and souls. More importantly, unbelievable things were said about how to heal them.

At the conclusion of the encounter, Norton and I sat across from one another, stupefied.

My first words were "What the heck was that?"

Norton patiently explained to me that there had been rare occasions previously when people experienced what I had. These people were able to retrieve information through a connection with another source, as if they are being taught or told things they needed to know. His work with others who have experienced a near death experience sometimes found a similar connection much like what I experienced. He then asked if I noticed anything while I was relaying to him what I said I was hearing.

"Like what?"

"Did you notice that you began to speak directly to me, as if the information and responses were coming straight from this person rather than through you?"

I had no idea what he meant and asked, "Could you explain that to me?"

He referred to a response near the end of our session. Much of the questioning and information that came through was as much about me as it was about Norton. As Norton was doing the asking, responses had been directed toward him specifically. The responses were answered by "someone", not by me per se. They addressed not only my purpose, but Norton's purpose as well. Since he was inadvertently brought into this "conversation", he had felt comfortable asking about things for us both. A connection developed through this exchange. Toward the end, he asked this "someone" what he could further do for me, knowing that our work together was not finished. He asked, "What can I do for Hollie?"

"She is in need of a guide such as yourself."

"OK, then I'll work with her."

The response through Hollie was, "That is good, because she will work with you."

Norton asked if I remembered this dialogue, to which I answered that I had. He then told me that during the session I had spoken as if the words came through me directly, as if a third party were answering rather than as if Hollie were answering for herself. He then suggested that maybe if we worked together, we would learn more about this connection. Was I willing to have another session to find out?

I couldn't help but wonder at the experience. I was pleased that I had recovered something of an experience from my past, although I still did not have a clear picture of what had happened or what it was really about. There were only more questions. Whatever happened, I thought, I was feeling great joy inside and for now this was good enough for me. So, I agreed to set up another session. I told Norton that I had no idea of how I could help him, but I was willing to find out, especially since most of the information that came through in the session was about healing. Not necessarily about healing a particular problem, but about helping to heal ourselves. Healing was spoken about in relation to our questions about finding a purpose, finding out who we were. Having not linked the two concepts of healing and a person's purpose previously, this seemed to open new possibilities. It certainly created immense curiosity. This was something we were both willing to seek more information about. Rather than physical or mental healing, the conversation had been a discussion about emotional healing. The dialogue that we encountered spoke to the need to heal the heart. In healing the heart, not only does it help to heal things about each of us, but it was stated that it is the only way to help others as well.

The indications were clear. If Norton and I continued to work together, this would be our area of concentration, seeing if we can again talk to "someone".

As the days after our initial session passed, a single question played over and over in my mind. What did this all mean? Norton, too, was grappling with the same question, although I was not aware of it until we met again. All I knew, in the few moments following our taping, was how good we felt hearing the information provided. Our minds were indeed open and receptive, but more importantly, our hearts were open as well.

When we spoke again a few weeks later, we discussed briefly what was said and "who" said it. There were no real answers to our questions. We agreed that another session would be required. Norton asked if I thought I could re-visit the place I had seen. I responded with a yes before I even thought about it. In the end, we concluded that we would continue to work together to find out more about the heart connection that sounded so essential for helping and healing. We've been working together ever since.

It was through hours spent recording every conversation I had with this "someone" that the Past Life Regression process Norton had been working with expanded into Life Memory Recall and a second new technique, Guided Light Therapy. Through information gathered in sessions together, Norton's techniques grew into what they are today. As part of our work together, we realized the importance of documenting the effects these new methods had on healing outcomes for others. In the next two chapters, you will be shown the impact of altering the past life regression techniques in order to look at healing in its expanded way. More interestingly, you will be able to see how the heart can be involved in healing; that heart healing can powerfully effect one's physical or psychological healing as well as one's emotional healing. While the concepts of tying emotional well-being to healing are not that new, what is new are the techniques by which this healing can take place. We will share the impact of changing the Past Life Regression technique by continuing to share the stories of people who have been helped and healed by the modified techniques of Life Memory Recall and Guided Light Therapy. We will also continue to tell Norton's and my story together as if we are speaking as one. Although we will be narrating future chapters from Norton's perspective, all information was cooperatively developed and his perspective is no different than my own.

*   *   *   *

NOTE: A few weeks following this first session, I finally found the courage to listen to my taped copy of what transpired. I say courage because it was odd to hear my own voice saying what was said. I was afraid of feeling like a fool. Even more so, I was afraid of considering any of it as real. Once I did listen, my fear evaporated. The voice I was hearing was my own, but the words that flowed out without hesitation and with such consistency and confidence were not mine. The manner of speech was not my normal pattern and the phrases used were not customary. Fortunately, the tone of my voice and the spoken words themselves were comforting and I found it easy to accept what was said. It was a challenge, however, to accept that the words were coming from another source, a "someone" and not necessarily directly from me. So at first, I just ignored this fact. I realized that I didn't have to believe that any of this was real or try to define who the "someone" was. I needed only hear the words and find truth in what had come through the experience. The experience could prove itself by any results that followed. And this was enough for me, almost.

Having been born with a good dose of skepticism, I did seek out information about what actually had occurred when I was 16 months old. I asked my mother to write to me, detailing what she remembered from this time. The reply came quickly. She said I hadn't been feeling well at the time, a bit feverish from a cold. She had given me a dose of baby aspirin, setting me in my highchair (which did have little painted characters on the back) while retrieving it from a kitchen cabinet. My sister, ever watchful, had parked herself on a kitchen chair to play with me, the baby. After giving me the medication, my mother had allowed us to play together while she finished a bit of housework elsewhere in the house. My sister and I often played with plastic cups and bowls, and this time was no different. Being a "big" sister, she would act like mommy. Whether she knew I wasn't feeling well or not, she knew mommy had given the baby something. So, she proceeded to give the baby more of the same.

My mother returned within a short time and prepared me for a nap. About 10 minutes later, she checked on what was supposed to be a sleeping baby. What she found was a limp and slightly discolored child. In a panic, she picked up my unresponsive body and raced outside to the next-door neighbor, my sister scrambling behind her. The neighbor was home and within minutes they were in the car racing for the hospital. It was only five minutes away, but my condition was deteriorating rapidly. I was turning blue, my body becoming lifeless. My mother remembered looking down and seeing that my little chest was no longer moving. She brought my mouth to her ears and found I was no longer breathing. My heartbeat was inaudible. At this point she was screaming for her driver to go faster. As she looked again at my small face, a froth had begun to bubble out of my mouth and ears.

Quite suddenly, a picture came into her mind. She remembered an article she had read in an edition of "LOOK" magazine on a new life-saving technique called CPR. With instinct alone driving her, she placed her mouth over my mouth and nose and just blew into them. She blew hard enough to see my chest rise with each breath. She was praying, with an intention that should have rung the heavens. This continued; one minute, two minutes, an eternity to her. She did not have time to even consider whether she was doing this right.

As she and I neared the emergency entrance, a first gurgle was heard. My color began to return, the bluish hue beginning to turn a softened pink. I had yet to open my eyes as the emergency attendant whisked me out of her arms. She would find out that my stomach was later pumped and my respiratory system supported. She saw me again when I was finally placed in a hospital bed. The doctors were there to give her my prognosis. They warned her of potential side effects, the possibility of permanent neurological damage or something called Reyes syndrome that is caused by an overdose of aspirin in young children. Wait and see was the approach. They would need to perform tests to confirm any problems. By the next afternoon, they shook their heads and said all was perfectly normal and I was released. To this day, there have been no effects seen. The aspirin, called *Liquiprin*, was taken off the market shortly after this experience.

After reading the information supplied by my mother, I bravely sent her my tape. We remain stunned by the detail I remembered and stated through the process Norton facilitated, the results of which proved very real. If this were real, I asked, then should I judge the rest of the information as unreal? I chose to accept it all for what it was and proceed accordingly. Norton did likewise.

In so doing, we opened ourselves to accepting that the work we would be doing together would require us to explore beyond the mind and body connection and certainly beyond the boundaries of our beliefs. We accepted all the information supplied on our first meeting and every session thereafter, concentrating on the messages of the importance of healing and the ways to improve the effects for others based on the work Norton had been doing. This incidence changed the work and, more importantly, was the first step in changing us. It is with this new understanding based on hours of taped responses from many questions posed to "someone" that we present the next story and the real-life results in upcoming chapters.

Chapter 7

▼

The Process Unveiled

It became immediately apparent and obvious that Hollie and I would explore what had occurred near the end of our first session together. Before embarking on this journey, however, I wanted to contact a colleague or two to ask a few questions about the process I was using, especially since it had already changed moderately from the original past life regression techniques I was originally taught. I was especially interested to hear what kind of reaction I would get after sharing the kinds of learning I developed from the relayed experiences that my private client sessions now revealed. I wondered how far off the traditional path of psychotherapy I had wandered. And I was extremely curious what they would say about the session with Hollie, and my asking Hollie if we could explore her "memory with someone" in greater depth.

As it turned out, the response was close to what I expected—reservation, lots of reservation of professional opinion. Unexpectedly, although the response was tentative, the overall interest was intense. Immediately my colleagues asked for more information. I spoke about assessing the work I was doing by the results that my clients were receiving. When I noted this, I saw amazement in the faces I was addressing, especially when I related past life memory experiences and current life healing together. I would hear, "Are you documenting this?" or "Are you sure?" Sometimes I'd get exclamations rather than questions, such as, "That's extraordinary, this could mean so much in the future!" Regardless of question or exclamation, underlying both was a general hesitancy in willingness to accept what I was saying as completely true or real.

Gladly, like myself, Hollie was not only willing, but enthusiastic to accept that what she and other clients experienced was true and real. She and I decided simultaneously, without complete acceptance from others, that we would embark on a mission to explore who was speaking to her, through her or from her. We would begin investigating what was said in the first session and those that were to follow through a series of questions and answers. Most importantly, we would inquire whether any of our work together could provide help or healing for others.

During the first few following sessions, it was clear that this "voice" was giving us directions. We quickly realized that we should have some kind of consistent process to follow for this information to be useful. I began by composing a number of intriguing questions before Hollie entered a hypnotic state. Many times the questions were based on follow-up curiosity about something that was stated in a previous session. Hollie and I had decided that it would be best if she did not see the questions I wanted to ask prior to the sessions. With this approach we felt that we would minimally influence the session. There would be no way for Hollie to anticipate the answers. We would get responses only after I asked the questions.

By the third session, we had the process and method down pat. Hollie could easily enter a trance-like regressed state by herself.[1] Once Hollie indicated she was ready, I would then begin by asking the first question on my list. I knew she was ready when she broke a momentary silence with a single word, "Begin." This process was the one that emerged, was completely accepted by us both and would be the one used that eventually led to hours of recorded conversation.

---

1. Entering the trance-like regressed state meant getting to the place of Light mentioned in the previous chapter.

Although our acceptance of the process was clear, near the beginning Hollie was still hesitant to accept that she was providing, in this extraordinary way, useful information about a therapy that she knew little about. Initially, the idea of retrieving information *through* her was something she judged as not possible. In time and with encouragement, the judgment was replaced by the realization that all things were possible, even the idea that she was indeed getting information from "someone" and the information was serving the purpose of helping others.

In order to reach this understanding, we discussed every minute detail of what unfolds when she is in the regressed state. Hollie did not initially realize that when she was responding to my questions it was as if someone else were actually speaking, not just relaying information. For example, when I asked a question such as, "Does Hollie know why she…", instead of answering using "I think…", she would answer using "she thinks…". All conversation, after the first session, continued in this way. I could ask Hollie about Hollie, but it was as if I were asking someone else. At first this was disconcerting for her, as I imagine it would be for anyone (in fact, our first few discussions were spent with me simply reassuring her). I made sure she knew that she wasn't crazy or schizophrenic, and she was not "hearing voices" in her head. I explained to her that she was safe in the process, and if she ever felt uncomfortable, we could end the session easily. I also urged her to not judge the experience, but to be open to exploring it as long as she was still interested. She could even think of it as make-believe if she wanted. As long as Hollie did not judge the information itself, she was free to explore the process as she pleased.

I explored the process, too. I asked Hollie what it felt like for her. She said it was as if she were just relaying information, much like you would if you were reading something to someone without a lot of interest. There seemed to be no emotional connection to the responses that came out. In later discussion, as Hollie and I became familiar with the process and method, she told me that the process was not without emotion, only the relaying of the responses had none. She mentioned that as she prepared herself, she would travel to this light place or the place in her mind's eye, and that on her way she experienced a number of emotions.

The first set of emotions included wonder. Hollie described how, in the process of getting to a state of mental calm, she would journey through a tunnel-like tube. This tube was very similar to the one she went through in the session that uncovered her memory of her near death experience. But even that description did not do the experience justice. As an example, she described the difference between seeing a leaf close up and viewing it through a window.

"The close examination allows a much more intense, personal, even emotional connection to the experience," she said. "You can not adequately describe the difference to someone without them experiencing it for themselves."

This held true about the work Hollie and I had undertaken. The difference between the telling and the experiencing was vast, a world apart from accepted methods and a challenge to believe. There was no way I could fully understand what she was experiencing. I imagined my colleagues feeling the same way when I described Life Memory Recall and the experiences my clients were having. I understood that for them or me it was as if to some degree, we were only peering through a looking glass, a window of unique experience. In order to get the "whole" picture, the viewer would need to have a direct experience. The good news is that while words were often simply inadequate to describe what was happening in Hollie's experience, they could provide me with a sense of how extraordinary her direct experience was.

When Hollie tells me that the colors are alive or shimmer with life, I can't really know what the experience is truly like for her. I can however, like you, get a sense of what she means by using explanations such as the leaf analogy above. The closer I get to the direct experience, the "first-hand" knowledge, the more I have come to know that the experience is beyond what it would be from any other perspective. As I proceed to provide more detail of the techniques themselves, I will use other examples or analogies similar to the leaf in order to provide a framework for Hollie's experience and our work together. Then I will try to relate how her experience and what we have learned compares with standard therapeutic techniques.

For now, I will return to finishing the description of the trance-like state as Hollie described it to me. Besides the colors and movement, there were other, even stranger things to describe. By the time Hollie experiences the tunnel, she has begun to go beyond sensing her body. To be more specific, she relaxes to a point where she loses the sense of "body" and travels inward into a void. What this actually is, as far as a therapeutic process, I will describe later. While I initially helped Hollie to this point in time, it was here that she acquired the ability to do this for herself rather than require a facilitator. This is an important transitional step in her process. Once she is no longer conscious of her body, she begins to travel in her mind. As I proceed, the descriptions will be a bit clumsy, since words are not sufficient for this process, regardless of how well Hollie describes the experience. For example, I use the word "inward" when I describe what happens once the sensation of having a body is left behind. This term is used since it is a common reference used in most psychological circles to describe a meditative or hypnotherapeutic state. It is not a specific reference by location or a point somewhere on the cerebral cortex, rather, it simply means turning off the external and tuning in to the internal.

However, Hollie would not say it is an internal journey at all. She actually describes it as a leaving of the body and a going outward. This is the motion she experiences. From my perspective her actual body never leaves my couch. Does my view mean it is not happening as she says?

The truth is that I can neither deny her view, nor acknowledge that it is indeed what is occurring. I do know that her body does get into a very relaxed state, usually to the point where there is no movement, and her breath becomes barely detectable. I have, with permission, touched her hands once I recognized that she had gotten to this point, and noticed a change in temperature. Monitoring them before and after our session, I noticed a change from warm to cold depending on the level of relaxation Hollie acquired. This change in temperature is a normal occurrence as we move between a waking and a sleep state. The only difference is that Hollie is preparing to answer questions and have interactive communication— NOT fall asleep. This change in her physical state can potentially be monitored, but for now, all I need to know is that she will remain in this relaxed state until the session is over, until she has answered all my questions.

At the point of this unique body release according to Hollie's sensations, the tunnel appears. Hollie then, as she puts it, leaves the body and travels along this tunnel or shimmering tube. As mentioned above, Hollie reports there are unusual things about this tube besides the color. She tells me that all of human history and before is stored there. While I was caught off-guard by this comment, I remained open and remembered that a person's experience can be anything they want it to be. All images are real just because they exist. I wasn't to judge any of it. This is especially important, since as I've stated before, I do not need to prove that the stories are "real", only witness the effects. What is important is what results from the experience. Had this been a normal session with a client, I would not have pursued it further. However, Hollie's statement had aroused my interest, and with her permission, I decided to explore it further. I asked her to describe what she meant.

She said, "When I go through the tunnel, I see moments of time and events. Like the way sheets billow in the breeze while hanging on a clothesline, the colorful bands within the tube bulge in and out. As they do, it's like seeing, for just a fraction of a second, people and places in the past. Sort of like taking a frame or two from a movie and splicing them together, pasting them on the sheets."

"Do you perceive anything from them, information or details of any kind?" I questioned.

"No, they're just there as I pass through. I don't perceive anything other than just see them."

After realizing that there wasn't anything more to pursue, I asked Hollie to continue her description. As she nears the end of the tunnel, she said that it gets very bright. The closer she gets, the brighter things are. When she reaches the end, she describes it as an opening that fills her visual screen with light. There does not appear to be an edge to the tunnel or a distinct point where it actually stops. The transition from the tunnel to the light just happens, starting as a bright pinpoint until it opens and fills her view. She said it was like driving a car and entering a deep patch of fog.

You don't know exactly at which point you lost your perspective of all the external surroundings, you just realize that you're in the fog, but in this case the fog is bright and full of light.

When I then asked her to describe the next phase of her journey, she began by telling me about the light itself. She described it as white, but was hesitant to do so, so I asked her why.

"This light is not the kind of white you would think of. At least not like any white I've seen in my daily experiences. It has an inner brightness that is almost overwhelming. No matter where I look within the so-called white fog, it is as if there is a light source of great intensity shining from the inside. Because this is everywhere and part of the fog, it seems as if there is a source of light that just emanates from the fog itself, from every angle or location. This creates a perceptual change that isn't like my ordinary experiences."

"How's that?" I asked.

"Well, ordinarily there is always an awareness of a top or bottom, a right or left, etc. In this bright light that no longer has any bearing. There isn't any indication of any direction or position. It is as if I'm suspended, yet I feel supported even though I don't see or experience what would feel or be like a floor or the ground under my feet. Try to think of it like standing on something firm while dry ice is rolling like a vapor along the floor. Enough dry ice and you won't see the floor anymore. Yet, you won't feel any lack of support for where you are standing. Whether dry ice or the fog mentioned above, it is everywhere and there is no such thing as floors or walls or any other supports."

Hollie continued her explanations. Again she tried for my sake to find examples I could relate to in order to help me gain a better understanding of her experience while also satisfying my curiosity.

While I was satisfied by Hollie's description of the fog of light (from this point on I will refer to it simply as the Light), and prepared to move forward, Hollie said there was more to it. She then went on to describe another aspect of the Light, having to do with the brightness. I thought that I had understood, and briefly restated what she had said, but she countered that I was still thinking in terms of light shining out from the center. She said that this was not what she experienced, and gave me an example to help me understand.

"When I said it seems as if there is something emanating from the center, I didn't mean it in the way of a flashlight shining out from somewhere inside a fog. Just as there is no direction to the light, there is no direction to the source. It is simply internal."

"Wait a minute." I stopped her before she had a chance to continue. "You'll need to take me through this one a little slower. What do you mean the source had no direction?"

"Let me try something and you let me know if this gets clearer, okay?"

"Of course."

"There is never a time during our day when light doesn't shine toward us. It doesn't matter if it's the brightness of noon or the subtlety of moonlight. We don't think about it, but light shines from somewhere and comes to us. I never realized or ever thought about this until the Life Memory Recall experience occurred and I saw something different. We automatically experience that there is a source of light "out there" and it comes to us. Do you agree?"

I agreed and felt my curiosity grow. I had never thought about this before either. Hollie had drawn my attention to something I had assumed as a matter of fact. This illuminated a boundary in my mind that I would not have recognized had we not taken the time to better understand her experience. This was significant for me. What I was learning was that I had a preconception in my mind about what my clients were experiencing as they related their own experiences, some having also experienced the Light. This was especially important to me because I needed to maintain a boundary-less frame of mind to be an effective facilitator for my clients. Only then can the healing possibilities be endless. This may seem like a very subtle point, however, I knew that it was a way to increase my awareness about the Life Memory Recall and Guided Light Therapy experience. And I knew that the more open my mind was, the better I could help others achieve the results they were looking for. So, I listened more intently, knowing in my heart that working together with Hollie was indeed already having a positive effect on my ability to help others.

Hollie continued, "Imagine that there was no light from 'out there', that the source of all light came from or emanated from and within everything instead. Each species, plant, mineral etc., had it's own source. Light would be all around you, mixing together constantly. Here's a funny little example that may help. When you were a kid, did you ever turn off the lights and play with flashlights? I did. And one of the things we would do was to stick the light end of the flashlight into our mouths. My cheeks would light up. In the dark, there would just be two reddish looking balls of light. Could someone really see the source of the light? No. The light would just emanate. It would look like the entire lining of my cheeks cast the reddish light. A person couldn't tell if the flashlight or the light beam it generated was pointing in any particular direction. Light simply emanated.

I know this may be a corny example, but take it to a bigger picture. Now imagine that instead of my cheeks, my entire being lit up. And instead of a reddish hue, imagine that what emanated was the brightest white light you've ever seen. It fills everything. This would be closer to what the Light is like for me. The source is not from anywhere in particular. It truly is everywhere. How's that?" Hollie asked.

"I think I see. Is there anything else about the Light?"

"Yes, sort of. I wish I could describe the whiteness. Just like I tried to describe the colors of the tunnel or the living nature of a leaf, I would have the same problem describing the whiteness of the Light. So I will simply say that it is alive as well. It is not shiny, nor is it dull. It is consistent, unlike the color changes that normally occur, i.e. colors getting darker depending on the thickness or thinness of a substance. The white stays the same white. It does so because there is no indication that the Light is limited. Therefore, it's like the white is endless in all directions so there are no thick or thin parts. The color is consistent throughout. It is quite beautiful, even though it is only white. A person may think that white is white but it isn't. And there's no better way to find this out than to go to a paint store and pick one out. There are so many possible colors, all considered a form of white. However, when you look at a white-white, you would see that many of the others aren't really white at all. You could easily distinguish the subtle tones of yellow or gray. The white-white would stand out for its pureness of what a real white is like. You would notice how bright it really is compared to the other so-called whites. Well, the white in the Light is like that only many, many more times the brightness."

I told Hollie I thought I had a good sense now of her surroundings. I think it is important for the readers to remember, that while this was occurring I had no idea what Hollie was experiencing. I had a small indication from our first session together, as "Hollie's Story" indicated. But, without this kind of questioning, I couldn't possibly know the personal detail of her experience.

Also mentioned in "Hollie's Story", she stated that she had entered the Light and "someone" spoke to her. At first I didn't really know what she meant, other than the fact that the mentioning of a "someone" had occurred in the life memory experiences for a number of my other clients. Prior to working with Hollie, I had never probed about what or who the "someone" was. Instead, I accepted whatever information came forth regardless of who actually said it. Interested in the information only, I had not asked if any clients had any attachments to or feelings about their "someone". I did not even ask if the "someone" was cooperative or could teach us something. This changed when Hollie and I began working together. I would learn that attachment can occur and later understood that this "someone" was very special to Hollie and was willing to answer anything we asked.

So what did Hollie say about "someone"? She told me that once she gets into the Light, she is still herself, but is about three to five years old. At this point she says she can feel herself as this little kid while still maintaining a kind of objectivity. It is like the feeling or experience one would have if they rehearsed for a part in a movie. When the movie is up on the screen, the viewers would see the movie unfold from an objective, external perspective. But for the actor who played the role, there would also be a subjective perspective, a full and closer connection. They could re-live or re-watch what they did IN the movie from both an objective (outsider) and a subjective (insider) viewpoint, giving the viewing a more personal, emotional aspect. While this example isn't perfect, I believe it comes close to what Hollie has described as being both five years old and her normal, adult self when she enters the Light.

Hollie's five-year old looks around and is initially alone in the Light. Then, fairly quickly, the Light begins to change. I will continue using the fog analogy to describe the next part of the process. Hollie describes the Light as organizing in a way that begins to take shape or form. The comparison I use is to describe what it might look like if a person in all white clothing stepped out from a very, very dense patch of fog. The edges would first appear vague, becoming clearer as the figure moved further and further out of the fog. Hollie agreed that this would be quite close to what she envisions, except for one thing. Although the Light takes a kind of form, it remains vague. It is as if the figure never quite moves out of the fog or Light. At this point I then had asked Hollie if she recognized anything about this vague figure while in the hypnotic state.

"Yes. It's obvious to me who it is, even though I can't see them like a person. There's no flesh or anything like that. However, it is as if it is the person without their skin on. I mean, if we have a soul, then it is the soul without the flesh. I think it's something like that. I can pick up from the image or figure all sorts of things that let me know whose soul it is. For example, I can tell whether it's female or male. Things like that." I interrupted, "Can you tell who, by name it is?"

"Yes."

"Is it someone from the past?"

"They all are."

"What do you mean, they all are?" I said before I understood what Hollie had indicated. She provided the following greater detail after our session when I asked the question again.

"The Light is full of people or souls or whatever you want to call them. In fact, the Light itself is nothing but souls, like a repository of life knowledge. It's hard for me to describe even though I can see and understand it so clearly when I'm there during the session. It's as if each soul of each form is still what it was when it was in human form, and somehow this information stays in the light. Not only does it stay in the Light, but when we're in session I can get the information easily. As the Light begins to take form, it does so enough until I get a sense of seeing the form itself. Otherwise, if it didn't take shape, I wouldn't know where to draw my attention because the Light is everywhere. By coming into a slight form, my attention is drawn to that area of Light and I can recognize who it is. It is as if, by taking a form, much of the human aspects of information return. I think this is done for my benefit, otherwise I'm not sure it would be required to be able to get the information. I think the information is there at all times, but this makes it easier for me or my mind to get a picture I can use. When the five-year old 'sees' the figure, she runs quickly over to the foggy form and wraps her arms around it. It might appear like trying to wrap your arms around a cloud. Once the five-year old does this, a major change occurs."

"Before you go further, could we get back to finishing your description of the term 'they'?" I pressed for clarification of the statement above.

"Sure. I say 'they' because the Light is made up of every form or essence or thought of the past you can think of. There's no separation. I kind of think of it as a big worldwide web of souls (something that holds the essence of a thing without it being touchable, tangible). Like our computer systems, the web connects everyone at all times, but it depends on whether the computer is turned on and what address you are linked to. Regardless of whether you use the information, the web is still there and knowledge transfer possibilities are still there. But if you're not plugged in or type in the right address, you won't be able to retrieve it. That's how I see it and experience it. The figure that slightly forms is particular to me. My mind has a connection with this past person, so I can feel comfortable and recognize this soul out of the many that are there. It is how I can begin to be a part of the whole. Like I said earlier, I think this image is created somehow for my benefit. So the Light is a plural place at all times and I just link to one particular address."

"Okay, that's good enough for me. You were about to say something about a change after the five-year old embraces the Light?"

"This is the best part, or at least the part I look forward to when we have our sessions together. Once I wrap my arms or the five-year's old arms around the Light figure, I fill up with intense joy and tremendous calm. It is as if I'm falling into the Light myself. I hesitate to say that though, because there's no real falling sensation or anything like that. I would use the word sinking, but that wouldn't be right for the same reason. Maybe the word is absorbed. It's not as if I'm moving at all, yet I am becoming a part of the Light. This takes only a fraction of a second to happen once I am filled with the feelings of joy and calm. Together these feelings turn into a kind of peacefulness that I can describe, but only in terms that make sense to me and may not make sense to anyone else as I try to find the right words."

I could see Hollie was hesitant about continuing, so I asked her to explain anyway. I reminded her that the experience is unique for everyone, so having anyone else understand wasn't that important. I was interested though, since I thought it might help me be a better facilitator for others and improve my overall understanding. I urged Hollie on by saying, "Please keep going. It means a lot for me to at least try to understand."

"Okay, but it may sound kind of strange. When the peacefulness comes or I just become peaceful (I'm not sure which process really occurs), I then know I'm part of it all. And when I become part of it all, an interesting thing happens. I recognize something in the Light that I couldn't feel until this happens. Time disappears. Space had disappeared in the beginning with the lack of location or direction when in the tube, but this was at first so different a sensation I recall it distinctly. I remember taking a note of the wonder I felt when time no longer mattered. It is as if everything "IS". I had heard about the idea of living in the moment as a stress reduction tool. By living in the moment, you find a kind of mental calm. I tried a couple of techniques to do just that. And they worked, or so I thought. That kind of calm seemed more like a mental calming than anything else. It was great to have as a tool and it has been helpful to me. In fact, I've come to recognize that anytime I'm feeling a little stressed, it's because I'm thinking about or reacting to something that has happened or could happen, rather than just sitting back and seeing what the current moment brings. So I know this idea of being in the present moment works to create more relaxation and calm.

What I didn't know is that I had never really been in the moment until the Guided Light Therapy session. I know the difference now. In my daily life, as much as I practice this great stress-reducing tool, I still have yet to get to the level of calm I can in the sessions with you. The difference here is that instead of calm, it is true peacefulness. And instead of reminding myself to only think or feel about the current moment, that's all there is. Everything just exists. Everything just IS, without past or future. The peacefulness I'm trying to describe is as if the moment is suspended forever, yet is still in motion. The motion is not a moving forward motion like we think of time on the clock, but it is a continual evolving. So as the moment evolves, it evolves into another current moment, not a next current moment. You are never out of the current moment. Again, I'll try to draw a picture, although it'll be pretty inadequate."

"It'll be just right, so please continue," I said with a keen interest and building curiosity.

"Let's see. Let's consider that the past, present and future moments are ingredients in a recipe that when they are put together they form a kind of batter. The more you mix the more inseparable the ingredients become until they aren't separable. They blend into one. Once blended, it is then up to the baker to decided what the batter will be or what form it'll take. The batter itself just IS. Well, that's kind of close to what time seems like in the Light at this point in our sessions.

What I can't describe is what the peacefulness is like that accompanies this experience. Even after experiencing this and having repeated this experience, I still can't get to the level of peacefulness that happens during the Guided Light Therapy and incorporate it into my daily life. The depth at which I experience being in the current moment in our sessions and when practicing mental calming or stress reducing methods are worlds apart. When I say there is only an IS about everything, I mean that there are no worries or thoughts of any kind that come up. Try and sit for five minutes and not have a thought emerge. This is hard, if not impossible. Well, when the peacefulness comes, every thought is gone and there really is only joy, calm, and peacefulness. These qualities emanate from everywhere and are a part of everything. They too are in a state of creative and continuous evolving. I liken it, for my own purposes, to being at the point of evolution before a thing becomes a thing. It is just an energy filled with the idea of creation. I bet these examples are starting to sound pretty lofty or completely absurd, huh?"

"To be truthful, they do, yet I believe they're correct," I answered. "Now that we've worked together I know you're not a person to exaggerate. Plus, I can't imagine what the kind of peacefulness you describe would be like." I laughed as I said this, never having been far from being the type A personality. Hollie smiled at this also. I continued, "I'd love to experience what you describe. In fact, most of my clients who have now experienced the Life Memory Recall and Guided Light Therapy process have expressed similar thoughts about the joy and peace of the Light. I have no doubt that what you say is exactly what you experience, and it doesn't matter whether I understand it completely or not. So, what happens next?"

"I disappear."

"What? I don't think I heard you right." I responded quickly.

"I disappear. What I mean is that the vision disappears. Once space, then time goes, then the vision goes. This doesn't mean that everything stops. I experience this as blending into the Light and space and time. It's as if I am an ingredient added to the batter and mixed in, inseparable from the rest and a part of the whole. This is when the real crazy thing happens. I become a part of the Light and am one with the souls or essences that are there. I can hear the thoughts, understand the forms and feel the emotions that are in the Light. These thoughts, forms and feelings are channeled together into one place and like a funnel are ready to be leaked out."

"Is this where I come in?"

Hollie smiled broadly and said, "You bet."

*   *   *   *

This is where the understanding from a traditional approach to psychological methods is needed. In order to look at what occurs for Hollie, which is now a familiar response during a Guided Light Therapy session, I've asked a good friend and valued colleague who specializes in traditional modern psychology to look at Hollie's description and interpret the process from a scientific or traditional perspective. This is especially important, given the common threads of experiences that occur with Guided Light Therapy and the potential it has as a healing therapy.

The colleague I approached, Cynthia Chase, L.C.S.W., I selected for two reasons. The first is that I have the utmost respect for her as a person *and* a therapist. The second is that she had an open mind and relentless curiosity about expanding her purpose in helping others. This expansion came after an experience I will let her tell you about. I think the connection between her experience and my therapeutic techniques will be obvious, but the ties to traditional therapy require Cynthia's expertise.

Cynthia's story, in her own words, begins, "Crash! My life passed before my eyes in a series of snapshots: mostly the peak experiences of my life, but some of the most traumatic, too, all in a matter of seconds. Now, I felt as if I had been given the opportunity to evaluate my life from an elevated perspective—with a guide showing me the most important scenes. "I'm glad I lived," I thought. "I am ready to die."

The car flipped over again and I was instantly in the presence of a bright light. I was embraced by an overwhelming feeling of love and acceptance, and I was part of the light. Rapture permeated my essence, my soul. Suddenly, a being appeared to my left: soft, ephemeral, flowing. Compassion and love shone through its eyes, and it spoke to me without uttering a word. "It's not your time." Another being appeared to my right. "You have to go back." My entire being cried out, "NO! I don't want to go." But in the next moment, I was aware of being back in my body. I was trapped, upside down, legs flipped backwards. The car was also upside down, and people were reassuring me that help was on the way.

Afterwards, I was devastated. I wanted to go back. I cried for hours, mourning the loss of my heavenly connection. I had been violently introduced to a new world, a level of existence beyond the mundane reality in which I had lived. My life would be forever transformed, transformed because this other-world experience had cracked the shell of my ignorance. I believe it had allowed me to recognize truths beyond the shallow physical realities that had completely defined my life up to that moment. Shortly thereafter, I began to consider two essential questions: Why wasn't it my time, and why did I have to come back? Eventually I divined the answer: I still had work to do. It was sharing the love that I had felt while in the light and bringing the light to others. How I would do this took the following form.

I pursued a degree to practice psychotherapy, a certificate in psychoanalytic psychotherapy, and another in group therapy. I received intensive training at Hunter College School of Social Work and at the Post Graduate Center for Mental Health in New York City. I went on to train with Alexander Lowen, founder of Bioenergetics Therapy. I worked in foster and adoptive care, social research, forensic work, and cancer care. I served as the director of a child abuse and neglect prevention program. Finally, I moved on to the work that would harness the love and passion that I have for bringing the love and light to others. For the past 20 years, as a practicing psychotherapist, I have seen people individually and in groups. This work, at least in part, was born of my momentary connection with the infinite.

I gradually expanded my therapeutic techniques from the traditional, medical, pathologically based models that I was taught, to an approach that now includes a holistic and/or spiritual focus. It is this dynamic, incredibly creative, and exciting work that keeps me so alive today.

While attending a holistic health conference chaired by Bernie Siegel, M.D., I met a well-known and respected hypnotherapist, Dr. Norton Berkowitz. Norton specialized in past life regression. I was skeptical, but fascinated by the implications of his work. With doubt, I began a productive and highly synergistic collaboration culminating in my training as a hypnotherapist.

I had agreed to submit to a session of Life Memory Recall and Guided Light Therapy with Norton as an initial introduction to his work. During the session, he focused on any physical problems that I may have had. He explained that chronic, unresolved physical problems sometimes have their basis in past life or past moment traumas. Ironically, I had had unresolved problems with pain on the left side of my body: from headaches on the left side of my head, left-sided neck pain, left shoulder, back leg and heel pain.

I offered this problem as an area of exploration in this initial session. An eager subject, I readily relaxed into a deep state of hypnosis. Reassured that I would remember the session, Norton also tape-recorded the session to preserve an objective record of the information.

Following a "walk on the beach" and other methods of imaginative visualization designed to deeply relax the body and mind, he brought me through the "corridor of time" to a series of doors. Behind one of the doors was the past life most responsible for my pain. Skeptical, even under hypnosis, I allowed my imagination to work its way to one of the doors. It was an elaborately carved wooden door, very old, very beautiful. I opened the door only to find myself standing in a field of beautiful, flowing green grass. I looked down and saw I was wearing an ankle length dress; my hair was long and brown. When Norton asked what the date was, I surprised myself by answering "1734. And I'm in England." My horse trotted over to me and I climbed on. I rode, full of joy and pleasure. Suddenly, the horse galloped out of control, and I fell to the ground, landing on my left side. The pain was so intense that I almost blacked out. I was full of pain and crippled for the rest of my life as a result of the accident in this recalled past life memory.

While still in the hypnotic state, Norton skillfully moved me out of the pain, allowing me to shift my point of awareness floating above that self in pain. He directed me to acknowledge that in that life I experienced untold pain, but that it was time to let go of it. My soul no longer needed to hold onto the pain of that past life. He guided me on a cloud and brought me to the Light—the same Light that I had experienced following my accident—what I call "the God Light." He instructed me to release my pain to the Light. The God-Light could take my pain, and my soul no longer had to carry it. With the snap of his fingers, my pain was gone. And it has been gone from that moment to the present, over three years.

That strange and mysterious experience has had a profound effect on me. Still wondering, skeptical, I searched for alternate explanations for my recovery: the power of the unconscious, the power of positive thinking, the power of suggestion under hypnosis. I did not know what to make of it. My recovery was contrary to my expectation. I could find no logical, rational explanation for the absence of pain. I expected it to return. It was just a matter of time. The intellectual side of me, the classically trained professional side of me could not accept the highly conjectural, mystical explanation. That by "imagining" a past life, then "releasing" that past trauma I would be healed of a long-standing medical problem that main-stream medicine couldn't understand or solve. My training led me to understand how expressing feelings about past pain could free the individual—in this life—but not in a past life of which I had no previous conscious memory.

It was not until the third or forth session later that my sustained remission led me to challenge assumptions about the nature of human beings, and who we really are. My experience in the Light educated me that I had a soul, and that ecstatic union awaited me.[2] Then I came to understand that the possibility that my soul was continuous exists, and that I have returned to earth many times over in different bodies. Further, the hypothesis was advanced to include that some of those past life experiences actually affect me in the present life. Of course I understood from a comparative religion course in college that many ancient and modern religions assumed reincarnation and the concept of Karma. Millions take the concept for granted and base their lives on the idea that they must do good works now in order to end the cycle of rebirth and remain in "Nirvana," a paradigm not unlike references of heaven. Previously, I found it interesting, but now I found it compelling.

I decided to enter into training with Norton, both as an adventure and as an exploration into these fantastic possibilities of understanding ourselves more deeply, and to determine the usefulness of these approaches in healing, especially for psychoanalytical use. My learning goal was both personal and professional. Although the techniques of Life Memory Recall and Guided Light Therapy sounded easily reproducible, I knew they were not and also knew I needed guidance to learn them. These techniques

---

2. The following "soul" descriptions and conclusions are those unique to Cynthia. Other's opinions and thoughts may vary significantly. Differences in beliefs do not alter the positive results one receives. I can say that more similarities about the Light and "soul" information exist than differences.

developed out of years of experience and as a culmination of information Norton retrieved from working with Hollie. I possessed neither of these perspectives and therefore, would need Norton's expertise in order to learn how to apply these techniques in my quest to help others.

Since that time I have hypnotized many of my patients. I have seen them speak in foreign languages, some of the languages reputedly long lost in history. I have heard endless adventures, sagas, traumas relived. I have seen incredible remissions of long-standing symptoms in my patients that the traditional methods of psychotherapy were unable to affect. I have seen eyelids flicker and smiles of joy when loves long lost are recalled. I have seen terrible pain and suffering released, allowing the patient to go on free of his or her burdens. For example, one patient with a long-standing Anxiety and Panic Disorder in which he feared suffocation and shortness of breath was totally relieved of symptoms following the recall of a past life memory of being murdered by his brother with a heavy barrel which crushed his chest. Another patient overcame a terror of flying (then drowning in the sea) through a memory of drowning in a tidal wave. By remembering first, then "releasing" those traumas to the Light as instructed by Norton, these patients are no longer haunted with fears grounded in events perceived as long past.

Two years after my own recovery, I have integrated Life Memory Recall and Guided Light Therapy into my practice, now bringing this particular form of hypnotherapy into my practice as a phenomenal healing modality.

My life as a therapist is exciting and varied, yet remains traditionally methodological. The client process still unfolds from the first session by gathering information about my patient's life, his/her background, and the nature of the problem. I find out about early family life, schooling, and relationships with family and friends. I explore whether he/she has been emotionally or sexually abused, whether they took drugs or alcohol, what their medical history comprises. I discover any symptoms or feelings people may be having that may have brought them to see me as a psychotherapist. I record their sleeping and eating habits, observe the physical presentation and mannerisms (body language) that help me to understand them more fully. I note how they relate to me as a means of validating or contradicting ways in which they may describe themselves to be.

Once we conclude our preliminary interaction, we can then go one step deeper. What is bothering you now? What's wrong? And we then launch into whatever conflict or suffering that has caused them to open up their life to a stranger—seeking help and guidance. The fifty-minute to one-hour session, usually one time per week, is the structure of our relationship. Acting as an expert on the human condition, I hope to offer insight and respectful advice on the issues and problems they present.

As the work proceeds, an even deeper layer of understanding begins through an exploration of the manner in which the patient relates to me, the therapist. For example, through understanding what is called in the field, 'transference', I may glean patterns of feelings about which the person may not be fully aware. Old patterns of behavior, attitude and expectation developed over the years in relation to parents, siblings and other significant people in their life, may begin to be unconsciously directed to me. As a therapist, I have found that pain, hurt and disappointment stay within our body, psyche, and spirit, unless "worked through" by letting out the hurt and releasing it. By identifying the maladaptive patterns that relate to the past, the person is free to relate to the present in a new way, not one conditioned by how they were treated or what they experienced in the past. This is the general theory and practice underlying modern, interactive psychotherapy. In many ways, this process is not so much different than how Life Memory Recall and Guided Light Therapy function. At the very least, correlations are possible. A significant and distinct difference between the two is in the time it takes to help someone heal!

Traditional therapy may take a long time. The deeper, the more traumatic the pain, the greater the "resistance" (another clinical term) to even go near the pain, let alone be able to release it. By the introduction of hypnosis, by accessing deeply embedded historical antecedents both in this life and in past life memories and releasing the pain and trauma, the resistance to a full and joyous life is overcome and a more rapid recovery is invited.

To further express my opinion about the pace of healing that Life Memory Recall and Guided Light Therapy affords, I would like to tell you about one of my patients with whom I utilized the process. My hope is that this will help to affirm the results of a shortened recovery process and of understanding the release of blocks interfering with a full, open response to life and optimal health.

I began working with Evan in June of 2001. He is a 51 year-old married man who gave the appearance of a rebel or maybe an unconventional cowboy. He was invested in his macho status and did what he felt he needed to do to appear larger than life. He kept his hair rather long in an Elvis sort of way, wore cowboy boots and leather jackets on a regular basis. A businessman with a wildly inconsistent track record, he moved from grand luxury to bankruptcy and back again. He spoke in a tough, boastful way about his violent exchanges with anyone who did him wrong, while at other times spoke with the gentility of a poet. He could as easily be highly sensitive and act as the ultimate gentleman. A man of contradictions, he flouted the law brazenly in certain situations then acted like Robin Hood in others, using his gains to help others less fortunate than himself. Regardless of contradiction, he was always the consummate romantic.

His track record with women, in his own mind, was a dismal failure. He was married three times and though the women he loved were good, at times he felt too good for him, he longed for his "soul mate". He desperately longed for the woman who was beautiful, intelligent, and a passionate lover. A romantic at heart, somehow he had arranged a life with his deepest need or wish unfulfilled. His present wife, a very good woman, was kept at a distance. Although lacking in closeness, my patient couldn't face separating from his wife "because she doesn't deserve to be left." He held her in high esteem at the same time he was contemptuous of her. He perceived her as controlling so he receded out to his boat or hid out in his business. When she tried to control certain aspects of his life, he had no capacity to stand his ground. He either flew into a rage or withdrew. Subsequently, in an attempt to make up for what was lacking in his marriage, he had decided to engage in a passionate love affair. Since two separate women could never meet his need for unity and truth in the form of a "soul mate", he lived in tortured conflict, alternating between guilt and feelings of entitlement. By the time he saw me, his loneliness was as intense as it was deep.

He was filled with regret, not only in regard for longing for his passionate soul mate but also for the fact that he did not parent his own biological child even though he had had the chance. A young woman became pregnant following a brief tryst with my patient when he was seventeen years old, an encounter from which a healthy child was born. My patient left both the woman and the baby when the child was about two years old and he has never seen them since. Within the past year, he attempted contact by writing a heartfelt letter to the person he believed to be his son. A response was never received. Although my patient helped bring up stepchildren, he deeply regrets leaving his own biological son behind. This hurt was so deep that he considered leaving his eleven-year marriage to join with his lover and have a baby with her. As strong as the urge to parent a biological child was, my patient could not abandon his wife and his commitment to take care of her.

It was at this time, with these feelings and a failing business, that this man decided to enter into therapy. Deeply clinically depressed, we would begin to grapple with his work and relationship issues. First, his business was in a state of collapse and he felt humiliated that he needed to depend on his wife (a successful businesswoman). Secondly, his wife, who was so good to him, loving and understanding in so many ways, did not provide him with the kind of intense and passionate images of relationship for which he longed. He felt guilty and at the same time justified in his affair because of this desire.

At the beginning, Evan's approach to therapy was cathartic. Simply put, he needed to unload, confess, and share. Later, he was better able to listen to a reflection of his own underlying issues. As those reflections flooded back on him, he was able to sort out what he was really feeling.

Through the psychotherapy he began to sift through the accumulation of events, feelings and experiences seeking to make sense out of a life increasingly felt to have no meaning. As he listened to himself he heard a lonely voice. He felt old before his time. He felt that it was too late, yet he was still driven forward by the need to understand the contradictions of his life. He began to speak of a spiritual vacuum inside of him and the longing to make an ultimate connection, to understand the meaning of his existence. The existential questions of "Why am I here?" and "What am I supposed to do while I am here?" roamed through his mind. In our sessions, he would philosophize, pontificate, ponder in poetic intellectualizations. The path, regardless of avenue taken, inevitably led to feelings of helplessness and impotency.

One month into the work I introduced Evan to the idea that it may be helpful for him to undergo hypnosis as part of the therapy in the attempt to explore what aspect of his history and background could account for his persistent loneliness, discontent and conflict. He was familiar and fascinated with hypnosis and by the concept of exploring his past. He was highly motivated to determine what the process could unearth.

He was quickly and deeply hypnotized, such that the first question put to him in that deeply relaxed state got right to the point: "What part of your past could account for your tendency to make choices that lead to your anger, loneliness and alienation?"

By utilizing the particular regression process that developed from Norton and Hollie's sessions together, as taught to me by Norton, my patient found himself in a recalled memory. He had long black hair, was aged twenty and a self-described "loafer." In a dark, candle-lit tavern, this individual sits alone at the head of the table eating soup and drinking beer. He was a stranger in the town, alone. Later, he goes out into the streets, "looking for trouble," but actually rescues a girl from being assaulted by three ruffians.

The next scene moves forward into the near future when the young man signs up as a soldier. He is in the same village when soldiers wearing red coats, white pants, and black hats with feathers attack the village. He fires a musket at an enemy soldier shooting a large cannon while more soldiers continue to overtake the village. The young man successfully evades capture as the enemy overruns the town in great numbers.

"I am older now. I am walking across a field carrying a tri-corner hat in my hand. My uniform is blue with long tails and white pants. I am remembering the battles I have fought. But there is no one in my life. I have fought a lot of battles and survived. But now I am old. I am happy because I led my men to many victories and I survived. But there is no one to go home to. I was always gone, living the life of a soldier. Always fighting. When I was younger I was a free spirit. I musta done somethin' stupid' because they made me an officer. But now I don't have a home of my own. It's time to stop fighting. I'll just have to go back to the family farm. No one is left, but that is the only place I can go. There is nothing left to do."

I gently broke in and told him, "You kept your freedom; you fought, you won, and you led your men successfully in battle. You had the camaraderie of the other soldiers."

"But," Evan breaks in, "I have no children, so it doesn't matter." Evan sobs deeply, suffering, feeling the loneliness and sense of desolation. "I sit on the porch smoking my pipe. I remember all the good times in my life. The rivers, the streams, the shared efforts. It was beautiful and I was free. I am now free but I am completely alone."

I bring Evan to the end of that life, to the time of his death, and he recounts it in this way, "I die an old man. Sad, yet happy to see the fields. I have a beard and I'm not so slim any more. I die in my chair just looking at the field, smiling. My spirit drifts away and all I see is black. Wherever I turn it is all black."

After some additional questions to help determine the meaning of the darkness, we comfortably agree that the man in my patient's recalled past life memory has somehow never moved on (whatever moved on really means). My patient refers to the man's body as the only part having passed on, the rest having remained, the essence of which is still with Evan today.

"I understand," I say, "the soul from that life is stuck.[3] A part of you hasn't been able to move on. It is time now to allow this soldier's soul to move on. Time to let go of the fighting, loneliness and alienation. Time to allow it to find the Light."[4]

---

3. My patient previously used the word soul to describe the man's remaining essence so I continued to use it with acceptance.

4. The understanding of "Light" was established in the questioning prior to my making the directive statement.

Evan responded strongly, "NO, I don't see any Light."

I persisted with my instructions of what I thought he needed to do in order to free his past life memory's soul and his current connection to it from persistent self-defeating attitudes. Speaking to him still as the soldier, "Your soul needs to rest, to go home. Seek out the Light, if only a speck of light and let yourself be drawn to that place."

Evan said emphatically, "NO, I don't want to go yet. I see the Light, but I don't want to go there. Everybody else is there. I am looking for another place to go." He hesitates momentarily and then says, "I am going to the Light and I am traveling very fast, but as soon as I touch it, it folds into the darkness. There is nothing. I need to be in the dark."

"Why?" I calmly asked.

"I have to help someone else. I'm not done. It's not just one person, I have to come back and help many others. I have chosen this and can't turn back."

"If this is what you must do," I say, "then let go of the 'fight' itself and hold onto the mission, the mission of doing good and helping others. Let go of the fighting. Let that be released to the Light."

As adamantly as before he responds, "No, it is not time for me to let go of the fighting."

This response was not what I expected and is the exciting part of the session for me as a therapist. I was reassured by the fact that Evan spoke his own "truth" rather than fit into a concept that I proposed. The individual truly controls the Life Memory Recall and Guided Light Therapy process. For me, this was an aspect that made this kind of work all the more fascinating. The past life memory or imaginative journey—whatever it was— fit like a glove into a metaphorical understanding of the patterns characterizing my patient's life. His own personal myth, from a professional viewpoint, included themes of service opposing narcissism, unity versus solitude. In that lifetime the preponderant ethic was service and solitude. In Evan's current life, the thread of narcissism provides a counterpoint to persistent acts of kindness and selfless behavior. In that "life," as in this one, he lived among people, but created a world of loneliness that was painful, yet proudly sustained. And the anger that brought him into therapy could be understood as a remnant of the fight that he wouldn't give up.

The fact that Evan's past life soul (as a part of him today) would not "go to the Light," speaks to me of the need he feels to make up for a selfish past. He feels the need to balance the scales before he can join "everybody else" in the Light. He is then subjected to a painful sentence, according to his own pronouncements, of loneliness. He is also attempting to free himself of his selfish grandiosity and do enough good to earn the right of brotherhood and love. What I perceive is that Evan, once again, in making up his own rules, is fighting the infinite love and forgiveness that awaits him. His past life memory appeared to be a direct reflection of his current situations. Life Memory Recall provided Evan with a clearer understanding and awareness from which we could begin to heal his conflict and longing.

Since that first conversation, Evan has undergone a series of regression sessions. They have led to an interesting transformation. In spite of his continuous pronouncements that he needed to keep up the fight one way or another, by accessing unconscious past choices from a number of past life memories, he was then able to choose with conscious awareness. Evan could change his current life by changing his perceptions about the past. Did he really want to continue fighting loneliness and alienation, or would he free himself to live in love and honor in this life? Did he deserve love and companionship? Could he receive love and companionship?

Yes, yes and yes! Evan has since terminated his relationship with his lover and has found companionship and love with his wife. He has come to deeply appreciate what she brings to him and he is no longer lonely. They travel and work together as partners, selling the business that had long drained Evan and working now to support his wife in the business that she had previously run by herself. He has come to accept his stepchildren as his own and at times even cries with joy that he has finally let in the love that was always there.

Evan has come to believe that he has a right to love. He has come to believe that those debts from his past, including any past lives, are paid. He is free to give up the fight, free to live. By understanding the constraints that he had placed on himself from that long-ago past, he was able to awaken to his present potential. **Life Memory Recall and Guided Light Therapy** provided an invaluable tool for elevating and liberating Evan's life. By accessing hidden influences that had debilitated, depressed and angered Evan, he was set free to be fully present in this life. This after all, is the goal of any therapy, whether traditional or non-conventional.

Therefore, my personal and professional opinion is that Life Memory Recall and Guided Light Therapy is a viable form of treatment offering an incredible addition to the range of healing techniques a therapist can have. Additionally, this form of treatment does not limit connections between the mind, body or spirit of an individual; instead it treats these holistically, offering a practical way for psychotherapists to assist their patients on the road to healing and the relief of suffering. It does so with expedience. It does so with open acceptance. It did so for my client and did so for me."

*   *   *   *

As Hollie had guided me to an understanding of the "Light" and the healing work that could be done there,[5] I was able to guide a respected peer. I learned that Guided Light Therapy could be taught to someone else, expanding the reach of its healing potential to more in need. And most importantly, I learned about how much of a person's healing and subsequent relief is related to what happens in the heart, in a place where no medicament can ever go.

---

5. This understanding took many hours of cataloguing details from the taped sessions with Hollie and therefore, is only briefly described herein. Technique instruction is planned following publication of this book.

CHAPTER 8

▼

GRIEF GONE BY

Life presents *everyone* with challenges. Of these, the feeling of loss can be the most significant and debilitating. No one passes through this life without some form of heartache. From my experience, this is especially true when there is a loss of a loved one. Once the person is gone, the pain of their loss remains for those that are still living. For people experiencing this kind of loss, words cannot adequately describe the level of inner grief they are experiencing. Although words from others can be soothing, the hole left in one's heart following the loss of a loved one is rarely ever filled.

As a society, we have learned to minimize our hurts in many ways. Pain relieving pills and therapies are convenient, numerous and frequently used. We humans, on the whole, do not like pain. We like suffering even less, especially for an extended period of time. In fact, we are so averse to pain that the management of it has become an entire profession. Some of this development has grown out of necessity. Diseases once fatal are now treatable. Long-term care can be administered in a way that provides more comfort. Life-extending drugs have been created. Dis-ease and illness relief has been and is aggressively pursued by science and technology. As our capability to understand the mechanism of healing has increased, our perception of pain and suffering has changed. We now expect science to solve many of our ills. Not only do we expect to find cures, but we also desire cures that have an immediate effect. In other words, we want anything broken, to be fixed and fixed fast.

This has led, as I have perceived it from my clients, to an expectation of quick relief. Emotional and psychological burdens have been treated similarly to physical ones. People want the pain to go away as soon as they feel it. An assortment of "not to feel" pills and medications have been developed in order to meet this need. For many, these medications positively assist an individual while the inner healing process takes place. They provide a comfort, like the way a pillow gently supports our head while it is the bed that supports our entire body. Used appropriately, in addition to therapy, this can be extremely effective. However, there is no medication that can fill the heart's missing piece. *None.* There is no immediate cure provided by science that can end the grieving of a lost loved one. To verify what I am saying, ask anyone who has experienced this loss. If you have experienced such loss yourself, then you already know this is true.

This desperate search for relief from grief has been a consistent theme for many of my clients. By the time they seek out my care and are willing to try something new and different, they have become frustrated and exasperated by traditional approaches that did not provide the "cure" or cessation of what ails them. Additionally, while many of my clients have had successful treatments for physical ailments, they have not had the same success for non-physical ailments. This group of clients continues to be plagued by annoying, even debilitating or ever-pervasive ills. Whatever the emotional, psychological or non-physical condition, the individuals suffering loss, especially the loss of a loved one, have been and are affected most profoundly. These individuals exist in a reality of unending sadness. It is a type of sadness that cuts through a person, an overwhelming sense of grief that is often silently endured, and in most cases left untreated. This is partially due to the impression that there is nothing that *can* treat this kind of grief. Medications can offer only temporary relief, while the greatest agent of healing, time, does it's work.

For anyone who has experienced profound, prolonged grief, this is a barely acceptable way to live. A friend of mine once described to me the feeling of her sadness after the loss of her daughter. She had died about a month previously in a random act at the hands of another's rage and lost rationality. The single act of violence was immediately fatal. When I heard the news of this horrible loss, it took me a few days to accept that what I had heard was true. It was so hard to believe. For the first week after the incident I thought continuously about this tragedy. I could not understand how my friend was getting up in the morning and facing a new day. I have always heard people say that under these circumstances you do what you do because you have to. But for me, I just do not know *how* a person does this without wishing themselves dead or wishing that the next day would never come. I felt for my friend as each minute passed, assuming that her moments must have felt dreadfully longer than my own.

When I spoke to my friend, I couldn't help but ask how she was making it through the day. She said, "First, there were so many details, the first week was a buzz. I'm not too sure what I really remember. Then after the people and details are gone, you find you need to get yourself back into doing the things you were doing. Although you may want the world to stop, it goes on without you.

I started back to work so I could concentrate on something else. My moments of realizing what happened comes to me in waves. Most of the time, I'll just burst into tears. Or, I'll be somewhere not thinking about it, and then the thoughts will come and I can hardly breathe."

At this point, I could see there was still so much deep agony within that my friend was only at the beginning of her healing process. There would be many more tears and moments of realization to come. I was listening to my friend as intently as I could. After she relayed a few more examples of what it's been like for her, I noticed that her eyes focused less on me and were cast downward. Her head had gained a forward tilt that left it looking like it was leaning downward. Her face became expressionless. Then she said words that I have never forgotten.

"Sometimes, the sadness hits me and my legs stop. They will not go forward or backward. The thoughts of my daughter hit me so hard they simply stop working. And wherever I am, everything else stops with me."

For days, my heart remained unsettled. This kind of grief, I thought, is grief beyond sadness. It is a time of hopeless days and nights. It consumes one's being to the point of non-recognition that other things still exist. And I wondered to my self, "Can I help?"

Yes I can. Or, more to the point, Life Memory Recall and Guided Light Therapy can. Past life work helps to bring completion to people who are grief-stricken and in mourning. The length of time one has been consumed by these feelings is irrelevant. Grief is grief, and until a person is able to release their sadness, it does not lessen.

Release is the promise of Guided Light Therapy. It gives a person the opportunity to "see" or "meet" the individual who has passed over in a manner different than just thinking about them. Through this work, people can enter the calmed mind state that allows them to visualize or feel a place where those who are living and those who have passed are together once again. They enter into the place of Light. As mentioned in previous chapters, this place is different for everyone, yet, when asked and with a little assistance, all know how to get there. Additionally, none of my clients has ever questioned what it is or where to find it. *They know.* I simply work as their guide.

From the sessions with Hollie I learned that, for example, while in the Light, a person may communicate with a lost loved one. They can talk to them and say last unsaid words. They may choose to express feelings that could not or were not expressed when living. The reasons why words were not spoken no longer matters. Arguments and estrangement have no meaning in the Light. All is instantaneously forgiven. What matters most is that anything left unresolved can be rectified.

Many times I have heard about how clients had held back expressing their thoughts and feelings to a deceased individual while they were alive. The reasons were many, and they seemed plausible at the time. However, once the loved one had been lost, the same reasons became meaningless. This has been said to be true by many of my clients. Often their grief is worsened by the realization that the things that had kept them apart from their loved ones while they were alive held no meaning after their death. The grief felt is compounded because the living person cannot undo what was done prior to the loved one's passing, and the pain of this lost opportunity holds the grief in place. It is as if the grief will not leave until the living person makes things all right again. Pain and suffering comes with feeling that it is too late to make amends.

Finding the Light provides hope for those looking for a way to say whatever was left unsaid. Sometimes it is a matter of just saying good-bye. This is especially true in the cases of accidental deaths or suicides. In such cases, it is extremely rare that individuals who loved those lost in these ways have had a chance to speak a few last words. This becomes more important as the grieving process continues. The desire for this opportunity can be overwhelming. The conversations generated by this desire are remarkably similar. Many clients have, while in the Light been able to express things they normally would not have. Prior to saying good-bye, most clients have a need to let the person who has passed know how they felt about them. When living, whether because of life circumstances or personal constraints, feelings held deep inside were not comfortably let out. Common unspoken phrases have been, "I care about you." "I love you." "I miss you so much." "You meant the world to me." All of these phrases can and are often said silently after losing a loved one by the grieving individual. But the difference between an individual silently saying or feeling things within themselves and expressing them in a Life Memory Recall and Guided Light Therapy session are profound. During a session, my clients can say or feel these things while they are *in the presence of* the lost loved one.

The majority of my clients have similar experiences when the session is to resolve grief. Once they are in the Light, it is common for the loved one to greet them. Often, my clients are greeted by a hug or a loving gesture. There is an exchange of 'I love you's. The loved one may tell my client that they are fine. Questions from the client to the loved one are often exchanged, and the answers provided are always healing to the living person. A majority of my clients experience an understanding that only the loved one could resolve. Many times the answers are unexpected. A new understanding is generated in this way, and for the first time many clients are able to view the loved one's passing in a way that finally brings comfort. Comfort in these cases is a cure. For example, in the case of a suicide, when in the Light the deceased may share the reason for their actions. More often than not, forgiveness is given and accepted. Whatever the outcome of the conversations, an increased meaning is found that is healing to the one left behind. What is needed to heal may be as small as one word or may be as grand as an overview of a shared life.

Life Memory Recall and Guided Light Therapy can help heal many forms of grief. It can help an individual find comfort when there is the loss of a lover, spouse or family member, the loss of an unborn child through miscarriage or abortion, the loss of a partner or friend. Grief from these circumstances can be equally devastating. The techniques work in the same way to heal all forms of grief. They provide a pathway to achieve the seemingly impossible—filling the hole left by loss.

To give you an adequate picture of what can be accomplished, I have included here a number of direct descriptions of sessions that resulted in the successful healing of broken hearts experiencing profound grief.

A client came to see me who had lost a child at a very early age. It was her youngest child, a little girl named April, and the death was completely unexpected. Grieving for this little girl went beyond the circle of the immediate family and friends and into the wider community. She was a child filled with energy and joy, well liked by everyone who came in contact with her. Her exuberance and joy was contagious, experienced by all that knew her. I, unfortunately, did not have the pleasure of meeting April. Instead, I had heard of the terrible mishap and the tragic effect her passing had upon her family and community.

It was April's mother, Yvonne, who came to see me. When I met her, I could read the question that she had in her eyes. Why? Why? Why? Why April? She was so young. She had barely even started to live. We talked for quite a while. Yvonne told me about April and showed me pictures of her. She even brought a tape of a song that April loved to sing. Yvonne seemed very happy to have found someone willing to hear about April. The pain of her grief was evident. We continued to talk about whatever Yvonne wanted to share, including how April, herself, felt about life and dying.

Yvonne was pleased to have found someone who did not try to change the subject to something more cheerful, as so many well-meaning people had. We did not try to avoid her grief and pain. We talked about it. By the look on Yvonne's face, I sensed that just talking about her daughter was relieving some of her burden. It felt to me like a slight opening occurred in an otherwise closed and suffocating box of painful memory. Yvonne truly enjoyed talking about April and the things she did. The more Yvonne spoke, the more the opening let out her pain.

After the conversation about April subsided, I told Yvonne what I believed I could offer additionally to help relieve some of her fear and anxiety, and lessen the overwhelming grief that she was experiencing. I shared the information I had about near death experiences and what people have said they experienced after having had a near death experience. I discussed the "Light" and where people say they go when they leave this life. I shared some information about the Light that Hollie had provided. Finally, I expressed my opinion, based on many clients' experiences, that people can go to this Light and talk to someone who has passed from this life, healing the heart and so much more. Telling Yvonne my belief was quite easy. I had no concern about her thinking that the idea was far fetched. It was much harder asking her whether she was ready to see April again. When in such pain a decision to speak to someone whose loss is so fresh can be frightening. I told Yvonne that Guided Light Therapy would allow her to get back in touch in a way that would help her healing heart rather than add more hurt to it. In the Light, remembrance is healing, and through this therapy it is embraced with welcomed relief. Yvonne agreed to try.

Together, Yvonne and I embarked on the session, going deeper into the experience until Yvonne began to connect with April. She began by calling out for April, then said, "I can not see her, but I can feel her."

"Would you like to ask her any questions?" I inquired.

"Where are you?" There was a very slight pause, and then Yvonne said softly, "I feel her love."

"Ask why she was taken away so early in life."

"I'm asking. Why am I not getting any answers? Answer me. No one wants to speak. Why? April are you here?"

"Is she coming?" I asked.

"Yes, but she is not saying anything."

Time went by in silence. Previous experience told me that in silence, for the client, the experience is still unfolding. When the conversational exchange stops, it does not mean that the session is over. Often in the experience of Life Memory Recall and Guided Light Therapy there will be moments when conversation does not occur, but activity occurs nonetheless.

After a few moments, Yvonne broke the silence spontaneously by saying aloud what she was saying to April. "Why are you so quiet?" Yvonne next described what was happening. She shrugged her shoulders when I asked. "She is little, as I remember her. She is wearing her jacket. It is the jacket that she had here. She is walking over."

"Ask if she is fully in the Light."

"April, are you in the Light?" Yvonne asked without hesitation and reported, "She is nodding yes."

"Ask if she is happy in the Light."

Yvonne again referred my question, "Are you happy in the Light? She nodded yes. She is smiling."

Yvonne's expression changed when she said this. Instead of immense worry and sadness, her facial expression relaxed. The pleasure of seeing April smile shone on Yvonne's face.

I interjected, "Is April with you, to some degree, on earth?"

"Are you watching us here?" She told me that April nodded affirmatively then smiled as if she was saying, 'of course'. "Why did you not stay with us?" Yvonne relayed that April just shrugged her shoulders again, without saying a word. "Do you know that we talk about you all of the time? What do you do there all of the time?" Again, the response was minimal and Yvonne said she was only seeing related facial expressions. I knew that Yvonne wished to hear April's voice, so I asked Yvonne to ask April a few more questions. This can often help to expand the Life Memory Recall experience.

"Can you talk to me?" There was no response.

"Can she speak to you at a later time?" I inquired.

"Can you speak to me at another time?" Yvonne repeated and then happily reported that April had said yes. "Are you still a child?" She answered no. Yvonne continued, "I think that for my sake she came as a child so she would not shock me. That is not really her form any more."

I did not need to question Yvonne about the above statement. For the experience to be helpful, it is necessary not to judge any of the information that is expressed, but rather continue assisting as a facilitator or knowledgeable guide. This then helps the person to continue accessing what they need in order to make the experience a healing one. Instead of questioning the information about April's form, I asked, "How do you feel now that you met her?"

"I feel good. It is like going to see someone and you go to their house. It would be good if she could come back here to *my* dimension. Because that is where I want her." Yvonne paused then continued to speak to April, "Will I ever meet you again on earth in a different form?" When I asked what the response was to this question, Yvonne said that April had directly said yes.

"Did you know that you were going to leave that day?" Yvonne asked.

There was a small pause after this question. I waited. Yvonne began, "At night when I was getting ready to go to bed I went into her room to give her a kiss good night. I expected her to be on her stomach like she usually was. When I entered her room, I noticed she was on her back, her big eyes opened wide. The window shade was up a few inches. The streetlights were shining off her eyes. She had a look like she was going to go somewhere. She had a look like she knew that she was going to be 'transferring'[1]. A wide-eyed look. A far away look."

I interrupted, "Ask if she can speak."

"Can you speak at all?"

I interjected without waiting for Yvonne's response, "Ask if April can speak to you telepathically, if not verbally."

---

1. "Transferring" was a term Yvonne used and I asked no further details about it's meaning.

"Can you communicate mentally?" April responded with a firm yes. "She's telling me she knows that I miss her terribly and that I should not worry. She is trying to assure me that she is ok. I should not worry too much about her. She came out to see me and be with me, she likes being with me but she has to go back to the group. She is not sure what to do. She knows that she wants to be with me, but there are people wanting her to come back into the group. She is saying the she could come back another time."

Yvonne quietly spoke a bit more to April, saying, "You have moved so many people with your passing. With your passing we found out just how much it has affected everyone. You had a way of touching people, loving came so naturally to you. Anyone that met you told us after your passing that they could always feel joy coming through you. You helped them feel the love they had inside."

Yvonne was beginning to understand what this really meant, that April's passing had a bigger purpose. Everyone that knew April felt her loss deeply. They felt it as a light that was extinguished. What was most important was that Yvonne was feeling this too, only as a parent could, but also with an understanding that there was another side. After an extreme and unexpected loss, after the grieving, comes a kind of understanding that is profoundly healing. In this exchange, I could see that this was happening to Yvonne. She was beginning to move forward, no longer stagnant from the pain of loss.

She relayed the information that April was sending her in a heart-felt exchange as it was occurring. For the first time, Yvonne could see how the people who were sharing her grief were also sharing April's love. It reminded me of other tragedies that have affected whole communities. Such events occasion an outpouring of love and support that is not initially evident, resulting in a gathering of people's hearts. That was what April's passing did. It brought out expressions of love among people who previously could not or did not share these emotions. April brought love to a community. April opened closed hearts. In that way, her passing had been a gift. Yvonne could finally see a meaning of great importance behind the devastation of loss.

There were many tears after the session, but they were no longer only the tears associated with loss and grief. Instead, there was a kind of relief or, more accurately, a kind of acceptance of what had happened. Yvonne described it, saying, "A vale of gloom was starting to be lifted." Other than this, she was a little unsure of what she had actually experienced. For me, I saw a distinct and definite result. Although hard to describe accurately, when I now looked at Yvonne there seemed to be a "release" showing on her face. By release, I mean there was a kind of tension that did not seem to be there any longer. The sadness that seemed to permeate Yvonne's expression had somehow lifted. This is not to say that her grief over the loss of her child was gone, or that her heart had somehow been completely relieved of its sad burden. What it meant to me was that the burden had been made lighter, and that the lightness showed on her face.

Time passed in silence after the session had been concluded. Yvonne sat there wondering what she had experienced. She was unsure of what to believe, and her eyes held a persistent, distant look. Knowing from experience that this type of delayed integration of the Life Memory Recall and Guided Light Therapy experience is quite common, I knew what to tell Yvonne. Simply, I asked her to just accept the experience for what it was, for now. I assured Yvonne that the experience would unravel and reveal it's meaning over the next week or so. This information calmed and soothed her. No further work was required on Yvonne's part. She readily accepted this information and left my office planning to come back again.

When Yvonne came back to see me for the second session, she seemed a little more relaxed compared to our first meeting. She mentioned that she had a better understanding of what had happen, and had started to realize why it was happening. In my work, understanding comes for each person a little differently. What remains the same, however, is that each client interprets the meaning of their experiences for themselves. The individualized understanding supports the healing nature of the recalled memory, infusing each person with his or her own unique knowledge of how to mend what needs mending.

Although Yvonne still ached for April beyond words, she seemed to have gained an understanding and acceptance that was not available to her previously. Yvonne was able to begin seeing April's passing as part of a larger, universal picture. With this understanding came an associated over-all calm that Yvonne had not been able to acquire since the loss of her child. Although calmer, she was very anxious on the day of our session as she looked forward to returning to the Light. Yvonne was ready to see April again. She knew that April had died, but her death did not seem as terminal and finite as she had felt it was at the beginning of our first session. This alone was healing for Yvonne. It was the first indication that her heavily burdened heart had indeed begun to mend. I knew at our first meeting that Yvonne could not imagine that her grief could ever be soft-ened. Now, as I watched her face, I could see that it did not have the grip on her that it once had. With that thought, we began our second session.

Yvonne began, "I sense that April is here. I do not see her yet. I just sense that she is here."

"Could it be that she knows that you understand that she is here, and she does not have to appear as she was on earth?" I questioned Yvonne in this manner, since I have learned that some clients do not have visual physical images of the individuals they speak to in the Light. As long as the connection is perceived by the person having the life memory recall experi-ence as complete and understandable, the experience remains meaningful. Many individuals do not directly experience seeing "vivid human form" when in the Light. Instead, people may pick up a sense of a particular per-sonality or character. It would be like recognizing someone by the way they walk when observed from behind, and the mind is able to associate the face that goes with the person with the distinct walk. The observer could recognize and have a picture in their mind of who the person was without ever seeing their face. In other words, from a single aspect of a person, they can be recognized.

Many of my clients have experienced this kind of indirect association. By allowing a client to associate a life experience they understand with a past life experience that they may not fully comprehend or vividly witness, the two can be integrated to provide a needed link. My background and my work with Hollie taught me how to guide my clients when such a situ-ation occurs and when the images appear visually vague. Having the right questions or suggestions to gently guide someone in these circumstances allows for a greater potential for healing.

Yvonne continued, "Yes, that makes sense to me. April, I'm back. Even though she is not in the form that she was before, I can sense that she is nodding her head. Time is moving on and our thoughts are with you," Yvonne told her. "We miss you terribly. Do you ever bring your presence down to us?" April responds with a no. Yvonne told me that April said she cannot do that any more. "She is on her [a different] level now. She is well received there. She knows the spirits that are there and she is very busy there. She knows what she is doing there. She is a little frustrated there because she knows that I am frustrated here on earth. She wants me to try to understand. She does not want me to suffer. She wants me to gain from her. She wants us to do other things."

I interrupted quietly, "Did she complete her task when she was here?"

"Yes. We do not know it, though. She was sent here with a specific goal. She was to bring love to every one. Everyone who knew her loved her. When she was here, she was working behind the scenes. Even though she knows that we miss her, she wants us to go on, to keep the positive energy that the community has, the community she was such a part of. She wants us to go on and not to get stuck. She had to go. There was no choice. We have to be here. We will be together in the same realm at the same point, but not now. We are to do our day-to-day stuff. We are not to visit her too much. This is possibly the last time to see her this way."

I said very slowly and gently, "Then be with April until you are ready to share your goodbyes."

More was said between Yvonne, April and myself before the session concluded. This part of the session will be kept private, although the reader can be comforted to know that Yvonne responded calmly and goodbyes were said with love.

After the session was over, Yvonne and I discussed it. The conversation began with her telling me, "It is strange that the last time April was completely visible. This time she was invisible. I was still able to hear her directly, sensing all that she had to say without ever seeing her."

This comment surprised me momentarily. Why? Because Yvonne was severely hearing impaired. We had worked together with great difficulty, yet, in our sessions with April, she had been able to rely on a sense that had long been mostly unavailable to her, thus making an indelible impression on Yvonne. To her, the ability to clearly and easily "hear" her daughter's precious and unforgettable words, instead of seeing, was something that opened her heart to healing.

I have seen Yvonne several times since our two sessions together. We have talked and reminisced about April, as well as our sessions. She remains much more at peace with herself and the loss of her child. Happily, she now knows that her daughter's life served a purpose beyond what she could have imagined prior to our sessions together. The loss itself can never be forgotten or undone. However, through her visits to the Light, a healing of the heart resulted. This healing gave new life to someone who was left behind.

Healing does not take place in just one part of the body or one section of one's life. Healing is like a pebble thrown into a pool of water. While it initially affects only one small area of the water, the waves eventually reach out, affecting the entire pond.

As a result of our sessions, Yvonne was freed to continue to love her daughter while allowing herself to let go. She was also free to honor her daughter's words and begin living her life beyond grief. Yvonne has since given birth to a new baby girl and I was privileged to be there for the baby's naming.

✳   ✳   ✳   ✳

The first time I saw Jack, I saw a man in his early 40's who seemed troubled, even tormented. He was overweight and looked disheveled. It was clear that Jack was currently so distraught that personal care was not his first concern.

Jack was referred to me by another therapist who had been unable to obtain the results Jack needed. The therapist thought that Jack was ready for something different, something I might be able to offer. So, with preliminary introductions out of the way and Jack's agreement to begin our work together, we quickly addressed the reason for his visit. His father had died unexpectedly when he was a young adult and they had not had an opportunity to say goodbye to each other. The day of his father's death, Jack was on his way to work when his father casually asked him to say good-bye to him. Jack was in an obstinate, rebellious mood that morning. He ignored his father's words and went out the door without saying anything. On any other day, Jack's behavior would not have been notable. However, it was the last time he saw his father alive.

Jack was devastated. He truly and deeply loved his father, and he realized that his defiance was responsible for the torment he carried, torment over the feelings of not having closure. Jack never got the opportunity to make amends for his behavior, regardless of the fact that his behavior could easily be accepted as a momentary lapse in youthful judgment. The irony of this fact caused him torment. The blame he felt over his defiant behavior only added to the torment. And once over the initial grieving for the loss of his father, Jack never stopped feeling tortured by his thoughts. When I met him, the torment had already lasted for years. There had been no therapy that resolved Jack's state of continuous anguish.

Needless to say, by the time Jack heard about my work, he was open to new possibilities. As mentioned above, he had been briefed about Life Memory Recall and Guided Light Therapy by his previous therapist. He was ready to go back and meet his father in the Light. He wanted to talk to him if he could and tell him that he was sorry about his behavior the morning of his father's death.

Jack easily found the Light and there he met his father. They talked, they hugged, they reminisced. As a result of this session, for the first time in many years, Jack acquired a sense of relief through the release of the feelings that he had held onto for so long. He had gained the completion he had been looking for: a chance to say good-bye. The experience and image of Jack's father was as real to him as if it had actually happened. After years of trying a number of things to alleviate his inner angst, within less than two hours, Jack found the relief he had been searching for.

I did not have another session with Jack. I knew it was not necessary.

About a year later at a social event an individual came up to me and said 'Hello'. I looked at him quizzically for a moment and returned the greeting. He looked at me and broadly smiled. He was in his early forties, nicely built and well dressed. "You don't remember me, do you?" He said. Embarrassed, I had to admit that I did not recognize him. He told me that he had seen me approximately a year ago. He did not give me his name. I could see that he was not disturbed by my lack of recall. Instead, surprisingly, he seemed almost pleased.

I suggested that if he told me the story of the work we did together, I bet I would remember him. He proceeded to tell me about a time when he was young and did not say good-bye to his father. I instantly smiled with recognition and total disbelief. The person before me could not have been farther from the distraught and tormented man that I had seen a year ago. He was so upbeat and alive. As we talked, Jack told me about the changes in his life, changes that began because of the tremendous difference it made speaking to his father in the Light. The sense of completion that resulted from our session had changed everything, big and small. I was delighted, especially as Jack went on, unknowingly describing the changes in his life using my favorite understanding of how Life Memory Recall and Guided Light Therapy work. Jack told me, "It [the session and its results] was like throwing a stone into a pond; the ripples kept on spreading. Some were big ripples and some were small ones, but all of the ripples were effective and added to my positive change." I continued smiling as I marveled to myself about how wonderful this work really is and how apparent its healing effects are. I reminded myself that what matters most are the results.

Repeatedly through the years as a facilitator of the Life Memory Recall experience, I have seen that when the meaning of loss has been understood and released, profound life changing results occur. The results demonstrate the healing potential, not the other way around. For example, quite often when I am conducting a workshop, some one will come up to me at a quiet moment, when no one is near, and tell me of a horrible illness which they had or have. They tell me how they would not wish this dreadful illness on anyone, and how it has changed their lives. But they go on to say that their illness also made them see life through a much bigger lens, giving it so much more meaning than it had before the illness. Some even describe it as a blessing, albeit a blessing often in uncomfortable disguise. It was through adversity and challenge that they had grown and matured.

It often seems that only through adversity are the greatest lessons learned. Only from hardship do we find true growth in our lives. Through Life Memory Recall and Guided Light Therapy experiences, people can gain an understanding of the true meaning behind this statement, especially when the discomfort in their lives obscures the greater meaning of their current circumstances. But this is not always the rule. Through my clients, I have heard of past lives that seemed ideal, even perfect. Lives of abundance, filled with all of the conveniences and luxuries available. Individuals living these lives had all of their needs met, so they did what they wanted to do. They indulged themselves in rich, comfortable lifestyles, with pleasure and enjoyment the primary goal. Looking back on these past lives, most of my clients considered them to be a pause in learning, even a wasted life experience, without substance or growth. There was no contribution to society. There was no effort to help others, or ease another's pain, suffering or burden. This kind of life was consistently viewed as non-productive, even selfish, contributing little to the evolution of the person who was experiencing the recalled life.

I found the consistency of this opinion surprising at first. Years later, however, I came to understand it in review of the experiences and outcomes individuals have come to expect through Life Memory Recall. For most clients, the lives with an identifiable cause of suffering, heartache or hardship, have been the lives that have allowed individuals to experience healing effects through Life Memory Recall. Conversely, lives remembered that contained no obvious lessons to learn or obstacles to overcome, had nothing to release, thus seemed to provide no healing effect. But I have found that this is not always the case. There is meaning, important meaning, in every recalled life experience. I have learned that allowing someone to experience a life remembrance without suffering can be healing in itself, because it can serve as a helpful reminder of what it feels like to a live without pain, illness or dis-ease. As we learned from Daniel's stories around his issues of alcoholism, he was able to begin the healing process by recovering the memory of a good life without the obstacles and challenges he met in his other recalled lives.

Upon learning this important lesson about the value of all recalled memories, often, in the initial session with a first time client, I will help them recall such a life in order to provide a level of comfort about the process. It provides a foundation for remembering what life was like before encountering the current obstacle or challenge. Once the remembrance has been gained, the client and I can begin to weave a story of healing in a relaxed manner, accessing the life memory or memories reflecting the current life problem with confidence and ease.

Although useful in the ways mentioned, the obstacle or challenge must still be faced. Life Memory Recall and Guided Light Therapy achieves results based on finding, then releasing a perceived obstacle. In most circumstances, this means that some form of undiscovered discomfort must be brought forth then let go of in order for healing to occur. Rarely have I seen healing be a spontaneous event.

Fortunately, Life Memory Recall and Guided Light Therapy are techniques that allow an individual to comfortably find what has been concealed. They can find a symptom, and the cause for it, even when the symptom may not be expressed or even obvious. Although it may mean uncovering something uncomfortable, the experience of discomfort is welcomed, because it can help my clients heal their lives, even of dis-eases they cannot consciously identify.

The following describes such a circumstance. I have included this story here because it illustrates a situation where the client discovered an inner pain that they were completely unaware of. This client had no idea that recalling a life with sadness and grief could affect her current life problem. In fact, as you are about to see, this client had not even come to see me for the problem that was ultimately healed.

Although the end result was wonderful, this section will require the open-minded, non-judgmental attitude required when assessing this therapy and its therapeutic effects. In choosing to include the story, I realize some people may be uncomfortable with the thoughts expressed or the subject matter, and I therefore, ask the reader to bear with me. I have heard many similar recalled life experiences from clients who are completely unaware of how common it is. I am not asking you to believe or dis-believe what they have said. I simply want to offer another perspective on how healing can take place. And more importantly, offer one woman's story as a message of how healing can occur at anytime for anyone, whether that person is fully aware of how to find it or not. Therefore, I chose to include this story for those individuals still seeking possibilities of their own.

Just as it is difficult for someone to re-experience painful events in their current life, the same can be true for a past life recovery. In the story you are about to read, the sorrow felt by the content of a client's experience during a group workshop could never be fully captured or duplicated by words. In this woman's voice, as she was re-experiencing the memory, was a tone of truth that left everyone tearful. It was evident that pain is pain and grief is grief, and it is 'real" when uncovered whether in a past life experience or a current one.

When the subject is grief, there are no limits. The greater the grief, the more the individual needs to be healed by releasing the grief experience. Finding where the grief is hidden is all that matters. In finding it and then releasing it, healing can occur. Sometimes, the stories themselves, if taken out of the context of my work, would be hard to face. Fortunately, under the protection of the Life Memory Recall process as the vehicle of discovery, grief can be faced. This kind of experience occurred for a woman in one of my group workshops. Her story was heart wrenching to all who were in the room.

The workshop began as they normally do and proceeded likewise. After going through the initial phase of a group regression, the individual phase was about to begin. A number of individuals had excitedly volunteered to work with me to uncover their personal life memories. Having decided by group consensus who would be participating, I proceeded to facilitate a woman's regression and asked, "Can you tell me where you are."

"I'm in my living room."

"What is happening in your living room?"

She proceeded, "I am practicing…practicing."

"What are you practicing?"

"Today?" she questioned, to which I responded, yes.

"Chopin."

"What is your name?"

"My name is Martina. I am now living in Paris."

"Where are you from Martina?"

After a very slight pause she answered, "I'm from Hungary."

"And you were practicing the piano? Why?" I asked.

"I am preparing for the concert. A very important concert."

"Where is it going to be given?"

"I believe it is an opera house." She paused briefly then said, "The Paris Opera House."

"What year is this Martina?"

"1935."

I repeated, "1935, and what's happening in 1935?"

"Oh" she exclaimed, "I only think about the piano concert. The concert is very important to us. I must be ready. I must be prepared."

I could see that she was feeling a bit uncomfortable, and there was a sense of anxiety in her voice, so I proceeded to ask a series of questions about her life instead of asking more about the concert itself. I learned that she was married and had two little boys, an infant and a toddler. As the woman became more relaxed, I suggested that we go to the concert. By making a noise with my fingers, I told her that when she heard the noise she would be at the concert. "What are you playing?"

"It is a piece I have written myself."

"Tell me more about what is happening at the concert while you are playing the piano."

"Well, my mother is very angry."

"Why?"

"I'm playing my own music." Her voice breaks slightly then she continues, "She wants me to play pieces she has chosen." Almost defiantly she says, "I have chosen to play my own music. I am a musician! I can play my own music. Can't she see that the people enjoy MY music, as well? Everyone's clapping; everyone's very pleased with my performance."

The defiance turns suddenly to a mumbling so I ask, "What did you say? Pardon?"

"There are…soldiers coming."

"Who's coming?"

With a shaken voice and emotions beginning to rise, she repeats, "The soldiers are coming."

At this point, I can see that the group of workshop participants had also witnessed the woman's growing emotional state. Rather than proceed directly to the next question, I utilized a technique that allows the person experiencing the past life memory to regain their composure and feel more relaxed. Once I knew the woman was more relaxed, I continued, "What kind of soldiers are coming?"

"They are very angry soldiers."

"I mean, soldiers from where? What kind?"

To my utter surprise and the surprise of the group, she responded in an angry tone, "You are a very stupid boy!"

Keeping my composure, I said, "You have the answers to my questions, do you not?"

"I have them."

"Can you tell me more?"

"Germany."

"What are the soldiers doing?" I inquired.

"They are doing what all soldiers do. They are doing as they are told…they are looking for us." I was about to ask another question when she continued, "My brother is a soldier too."

"Your brother is a soldier too—with what army?"

"At home my brother is a soldier, at home."

"In Hungary?"

"Yes," she said flatly.

"And what happens now? Do the soldiers find you? Or not?"

Barely audible, she said, "No, not now. I am protected at this time. I am protected. I am…I am a musician."

"Uh hmm. So the soldiers don't bother you now."

Her voice grew louder. "Oh, they frighten me, they make me very angry, but they do nothing." The woman's voice broke as she provided this answer. I also noted, that the group had moved closer during the last round of questions. Just as the woman became moved, so did the small group around her. There was something in her voice that registered with everyone. The break in her voice seemed to be a precursor of something heartfelt underneath. Until now, there had been nothing in her responses to indicate this yet, everyone in the room had a sense that this was true. It was here that I would facilitate the process of deepening the past life memory experience. I also knew, that from this point forward we would be discovering what was needed for some kind of healing to occur.

I proceeded by giving the woman instructions to move to a point of time in this life that was most important to her. With a snap of my fingers she would be there. "Tell me what is happening."

Before answering, the woman began to cry. Through tears she said, "It is very frightening—there are people everywhere. There are guns everywhere. People are screaming and everything is burning. I'm trying to find my babies. Where are my babies?"

The woman's cries became the cries of a mother stricken with loss. This kind of grief has a sound all its own. It was a sound that penetrated the room. The workshop participants, upon hearing the woman's sobs, shed tears of their own. I hesitated for a moment, deciding whether to end or continue the session. The group silently urged me to continue. For the woman herself, I knew I had to continue, for her benefit. During the time it took me to have these thoughts, the woman's sadness opened into deep grief, as she said, "My babies...are burning!"

I quickly uttered the words that would bring relaxation back to the woman. Once calmed, I ask her if she could tell me what had happened during the rest of her life.

She cried out, "I was not home."

"Did the soldiers do this, or what?"

"Who knows how these things begin? Who knows...(Fading). I, my family is all gone. I...will not...play for them."

"Who is 'them'?"

In a whisper, "The Germans." Then she repeated, "I will not play for them."

"Do they ask you to?"

"Oh yes." She paused then said, "They must be entertained."

"What is your full name?"

"It is a name my mother has chosen. My name is Martina…Martina Slovonsky." (The spelling is phonetic, based on the taped recording produced during the session.)

"Where are you when they ask? And what do they do when you say no, you will not play for them?" I inquired.

"In a place like a police station. They would hit me. They will become very angry." Once again the woman's voice became defiant and strong. "I will not play…anymore. I will not play. They have taken my babies away."

Once she said this, the woman's voice again broke and she began to moan. Her speech was becoming inaudible and broken as well. "Away. I never…" she began to sob, "I never…I, I…who is safe…who was saved.

As difficult as it was to have the woman continue,[2] I knew that she was approaching the point of rediscovering something that she needed. I knew that she would not want me to stop helping her finish this life. The group was gripped by the woman's sobs. They, too, needed resolution, since their hearts' and the woman's were now one with the experience. So I continued, very gently, "Talk to me, tell me. I know it's hard to say, but tell me what is happening."

Completely sobbing, "Why…would they…take away…two little boys? So small…so wrong…"

"Is your husband with you?"

"Gone…gone. All gone."

"What did they do with you?"

The woman let out a deep, slow breath then said, "Why does it matter?"

---

2. There are signs I watch for and questions I ask to ensure that a session never goes beyond a client's comfort level. This was done prior to proceeding with the session.

"This will help you now, that's why it matters. That's the only reason it matters, to make life better for you now. Can you tell me, what do they do with you?"

Clearly struggling and with a whimper she said, "I am to be taken away."

"To be taken away? Do you know where they will take you?"

"Some place away from Paris."

"Away from Paris—is it in France or elsewhere? How do you travel there?"

As if defeated she simply stated, "You could never imagine."

"Tell me if you can."

"After we have been discharged from the station, we are walking…it is very cold there…long pause…it is hard to imagine…it is hard to imagine what they are thinking. We are people. We are…walking"

"Where do you walk to?"

"There is a bus and we will walk to the bus. Then there is a train."

"Do you go on the train?"

Her voice trembled, "Yes. We have no choices. It is very, very cold. There are no seats on this train."

Using the technique mentioned previously, I prompted her to go to the end of her destination. "Where are you?"

The inhuman wail that followed felt like a shockwave hitting the group. "It's very crowded, so many people, so many people…"

"Where are all these people?"

"In a room, it's just a room. I don't know where we are." Her breathing became labored, as if she were in pain.

"What are all the people doing? What is happening?"

In between breaths she said, "Everyone is very frightened."

"Very frightened," I repeated.

"I am happy."

Shocked and taken aback, I asked, "You're happy…why?"

Without any sadness in her tone and a now relaxed body she said, "I know I will die in this place."

"Why does that make you happy? Tell me why you are smiling now."

"The children are with me."

"Yes, the children are with you. Do you also know that you will always have contact with them, now and at future times?"

"Yes."

"Do you know you are with them in spirit?"

"Yes."

"And you can leave the pain and suffering behind? Just take the love with you." She nodded affirmatively, so I continued, "As time goes on you may leave more and more behind and take more and more love with you. All right? Can you do that?"

"Yes."

At this point, I began to guide the woman back from her past life memory and into the present. There are a number of techniques to do this, each depending upon a client's particular situation. Each technique was developed to enhance the client's experience such that it will be the most beneficial for the individual and their future understanding.

"You will leave all the sadness and grief of that life behind and only bring back the love with you. 1, 2...you will feel really terrific, you will have full understanding, full recall but only in an emotionally positive way. You know what happened in the past and you are going to leave it there, 3...4. When we get to 5 you will be relaxed and back where we started, still calm and relaxed...5. Before you open your eyes, do you wish to share anything with us?" I inquired. "If you'd rather not its perfectly all right."

A lengthy pause followed. Often when a past life memory is filled with emotion, the client experiences much more than they say. Their minds comprehend the whole experience. For this woman, it was obvious that due to the overwhelming grief she experienced, her responses were minimal. However, the simple sentences she uttered had had a profound effect on everyone who participated in the workshop. After tears were shared in the process, a kind of release happened as well, for the woman and the remainder of the group. All hearts had been opened in compassion, for oneself and for all.

I was allowing the woman time to fully collect her thoughts, when suddenly she blurted out prior to opening her eyes, "In the room...after a while you just can't breathe anymore."

"Uh hmm," was all that I could mutter.

"We can leave. You leave because you are dead...your body cannot work without air so you leave. Not your body, but *you* leave." There was again a brief pause then, "There is no air left in the room."

I knew we were at the point of finding the meaning, or part of the meaning, of the past life memory. This is the point in a session when understanding of the past starts and healing of the current life begins. Therefore, I asked, "In this life do you have a problem breathing?"

"Sometimes."

"Why?"

"Sometimes I have no air."

"You realize that that happened in a past life, do you not? And you are not to take it back into this life, your current life?" I allowed for a short pause then prompted the woman for a response by asking, "Do you understand that?"

"I understand."

"Can you do that? Can you leave all those sad and negative things back in the past life where they belong?"

"Breathing...I have tried to do that," she finally said. "I have tried, yes."

"And has it worked for you?"

"Sometimes."

"Is there anything positive you can bring back from that past life...love of children? Can you take that back with you now? Love of life? Can you leave the negative behind? Can you leave the room with no air behind?"

Sobbing...

"Can you leave the negative there?"

Sobbing...

"TRY. That happened in the past life, not in this one. Leave it there. Let yourself be well in this one."

Still sobbing without response.

"Take back the love of the children and leave all the rest behind, ok? Can you now let go of it and do that?"

Finally an answer came, "Yes, yes I can."

"Good. Leave the difficult time of breathing back there. Leave the death back there, leave everything back there, except the love. Take back the love. Can you do all of that?"

"Yes, I can."

And so with that ending statement and a tiny bit of direction, the woman opened her eyes. Very little was said after that. The workshop concluded with a few questions about the process and a few comments about the impact of the session. I verified that everyone, including the woman, felt good about what had happened, and I shared my thoughts on the session. Although emotionally painful to experience and witness, everyone left feeling better than when they came in. The overall thought was that something was gained in the process and that time would tell what it was and whether it was healed or not. Regardless of knowing the scope of the results, all agreed when departing that their hearts were filled to the brim with love and this in itself was healing to all.

For the woman, healing took no time at all. Yet, I would not be aware of her healing until three years later. One day, I accidentally ran into her. After a short exchange, I recalled vividly the experience that had occurred in my workshop three years earlier. Because of the emotion involved, it was an experience I could not forget, nor did I want to. I asked how she was feeling, meaning it in a general sense.

She responded with confidence, "My asthma is still gone."

"Your what?"

"The breathing problem I mentioned to you after our session, it was asthma. Like you said, I could leave it behind and I did. I have not had asthma since your workshop."

All I could say was, "How wonderful!" I was thinking, "But of course". Every time I forget about the potential of the kinds of possible healing with Life Memory Recall and Guided Light Therapy, something happens that confirms what I know. And what I know is that whatever the experience is that a person encounters, it is exactly what they need to have healing results.

Sometimes that experience is full of past sadness or grief. Sometimes the experience comes from current sadness or grief. Either way, grief is grief and without healing, it makes life unbearable.

The essence of the sadness or grief may vary, perhaps representing a form of loss, separation, guilt or another difficulty to be challenged and overcome. The ability of Life Memory Recall to be able to address any moment of the past and any circumstance without judgment allows the experience to become a healing one. Many people come to see me expressing a general sadness, a kind that has no direct link to any specific incidence or event. Often, the search for answers to resolve the sadness has been long. They come to my office with great frustration at not having found a reason for their lingering feelings. Or, conversely, people will think they can identify the cause of their sadness exactly, only to discover they are mistaken. In fact, some individuals are so sure that they know the reason, they will spend a great deal of time describing their problems and the reason for it when we start our work together: when it started, what provoked it and why they have it. Yet, as we continue our work together, these reasons are rarely the sole cause and contributor to their heart's discomfort or their body's ailments.

For the purposes of self-protection, avoidance of pain, to decrease suffering or to not feel grief, human beings are capable of rationalizing their reality in ways designed to minimize hurt. This is neither good nor bad. It is just a fact of how I have seen things work in my years as a therapist. People may decide that a particular issue is the cause for their sadness, even though the root cause is an entirely different issue, one less socially acceptable to discuss. It is certainly easier to place the blame on a problem that fits into an acceptable category, both for the sufferer and others.

When a person's pain or suffering stems from events difficult to talk about, alternative means to discuss and release the events are sometimes preferred. I have seen many clients desiring release from the burdens caused by experiences of molestation, sexual abuse, rape or abortion. These individuals felt their issues were "talk taboos", and therefore, could not find resolution of their pain and suffering through traditional means of healing and treatment.

Life Memory Recall and Guided Light Therapy allow the words that need to be spoken to come forth. In so doing, the hurt from such injuries can be released and healed. It may take some time with my clients to find the root issue that needs to be revealed, but it is only when this "hidden piece" is uncovered that healing begins. And it does not matter whether the hidden pieces are from a person's current life or a recalled life memory. It is important to note that if I see my clients experiencing great discomfort in finding their pieces, it can be minimized by the techniques I have developed. Never in the process is more pain, suffering, sadness or grief added to a client's current burden. Instead, they find the ability to face the experience and release it, lightening the burden so healing can be completed.

My clients have told me that once the missing piece or issue surfaces, especially when in a recalled life memory, they are often surprised by the stories that entered into their awareness, yet, something inside them felt as if they knew that it should. The relief of finally letting go in the present moment makes the discovery worthwhile. Working through the heart in this way, as learned from Hollie and her special "someone", many, many of my clients have been relieved of the burdens they carried.

CHAPTER 9

▼

IN THE LIGHT OF
UNDERSTANDING

There is no right way or wrong way to think or feel about Life Memory Recall and Guided Light Therapy. Given that our daily lives seem filled with rights and wrongs, this alone is good news. It means we are free to *not* judge these techniques. We all have our own shoes to walk the path of life. Wearing someone else's is not an option. Each life memory is as unique as we are. The meaning acquired remains an individual understanding. How this meaning is then applied can only be one of personal revelation. There is truly no right way or wrong way to perceive another person's experience. The individual person determines the benefits received by these techniques. Others can only confirm the benefits, as they witness the healing that takes place.

Why Life Memory Recall or Guided Light Therapy works the way it does may never be fully understood. However, *what* it does can be understood by comparing the similarities and differences from personal journeys taken, each person having sought out this work as a means of healing. As the stories in this book have indicated, healing itself is hard to define. Given the difficulty in defining what healing means and the differences in the life memory experiences alone, make it impossible to clearly say who has been healed and who hasn't.

It is easy to say someone has been healed when they experience relief from a particular ailment that otherwise had not improved through methods previously employed. It is easy in these cases because there is something measurable. Indicators exist that can be monitored and evaluated by traditional means. In fact, as science expands its understanding of the human body, more measures are being created allowing for better evaluation of the human condition. No longer confined to the body and our physiologic workings, science itself is assisting in making Life Memory Recall and Guided Light Therapy more acceptable. It is doing so by furthering our understanding that the human being is a many-layered creature, and dis-ease and illness cannot be separated from the entire being as merely physiological expressions.

Our emotions, our behavior, and our perceptions of our inner world, as well as the forces we believe guide us, are now considered significant factors for the understanding of the dis-ease process. A simple and common example can be found among the wealth of information about stress and the adverse biochemical events it causes in the body. This is a shift in thinking. It allows us to consider our emotional well being as a contributing factor to our physical well being. What this information has done is open a pathway for new thoughts. It is no longer absurd to say that how we react to things or perceive our experiences can have an effect on our bodies. In other words, what we experience and what we think may indeed affect our bodies in significant ways. We may treat our bodies well, yet if our thoughts are disturbing to us, the body may still respond negatively regardless of our efforts to care for it.

Life Memory Recall and Guided Light Therapy are means to deepen our connection to thoughts otherwise hidden. They allow for the opportunity to find out what we may be thinking and how this thinking has an effect in our lives. Additionally, they allow us to create the pictures that represent inner feelings so that our mind has something tangible to work with. Without the pictures of our heart's response, we are left with feelings. These feelings can then run rampant, sometimes overriding our thoughts in such a way that our body is adversely affected. As we explore the pictures created, we also have the opportunity to release any meaning associated with them that creates a limitation to our well being. In finding greater well being, the result is less inner stress and a decrease in the bio-chemical events that cause dis-ease in the body.

When I started my work as a past life therapist, merely stating this concept would have amounted to putting my neck out professionally. Now I can say it with confidence and the backing of scientific research.

To provide even greater evidence for the healing work Hollie and I are doing, I contacted a cardiologist I knew. My intention was to discuss with him the mind, emotion and body relationship to dis-ease or healing as I experienced it from working with my clients. I believed he would be open to listening to my thoughts about the healing that takes place with Life Memory Recall and Guided Light Therapy. After a lengthy discussion, I asked him if he would be willing to begin doing some research with these techniques. Happily, he agreed.

H. Robert Silverstein, M.D., F.A.C.C., a cardiologist and internist, provided me with an understanding of the parameters of the research. We had decided that we would begin with patients or clients with asthma. We agreed on asthma because from my perspective, it was a condition relatively easy to work with, and from his, it was a dis-ease state that was relatively easy to assess. We would utilize the tool of measuring peak flow rates (breathing capacity) and the levels of medication(s) individuals required to alleviate their asthmatic symptoms or suppress their condition as our experimental parameters. It was important that the research be simple, straight forward and quantifiable in order to measure the healing effects of my therapy.

The following are a few condensed and edited examples of the kinds of past life memories discovered that have had related healing results, in particular, to breathing and asthma related problems.

• A Roman legionnaire who was stabbed in the chest with a sword died as his lungs filled with blood and his ability to breathe was choked off.

- A miller worked in an old wind-mill grinding grain into flour for many years, breathing in the dust that was in the air. After years of breathing in the flour dust his lungs filled and became congested. Breathing became very difficult.

- A young boy was swimming and was pulled down by the undertow. He fought desperately, but he could not reach the surface. His lungs filled with water and he drowned.

- A woman was in the kitchen making a birthday cake for her son's party when the gas oven malfunctioned and she was asphyxiated.

The list of possible 'cause' scenarios is virtually endless: their meaning for healing outcomes just as numerous. The cause could be things that have occurred in a past life where the breathing had been affected, in turn, contributing to the symptoms of asthma in this life. When the relationship of the current expression of asthmatic symptoms and past life memories are directly linked through the Life Memory Recall process, the health problems associated with the breathing symptoms are relatively easy to release and permit the individual to be free of continued asthmatic reactions.

However, not all past life memory causes of asthma are as simple and directly related as the examples given above. While the expression of asthmatic symptoms may be related to past life memories, they may not have obvious connections to breathing difficulties. In those memories, asthma-like problems are often attached to fear, guilt, loss of love, and other unexpected reasons. This indirect connection, manifesting itself as breathing problems, remains completely hidden to my clients prior to our sessions together. With the help of Life Memory Recall and Guided Light Therapy, these problems can be located and identified. Once they are located and identified, the individual can release them and let the healing occur.

Below are excerpts of the notes from the asthma research project with Dr. Silverstein. All of the client sessions are taped from the time the client begins until our sessions end. For these individuals, the "past" can refer to a past remembrance from the individual's current life or a memory of a past life previously lived. The case studies provided herein are summarized and are specific to the effects on asthma. The summaries do not however, provide all the detail of the method used; the right questions to ask, the signs to know where someone is in the process, or the actual technique used to retrieve a past life memory or guide someone in the Light (this aspect of the sessions would require too much tutelage in technique to be of benefit for the purpose here). The number of sessions involved for this project varied by individual, ranging between three to six sessions total. Some clients have seen phenomenal healing results with only one session, while others have needed many. Again, as I have repeatedly reminded the reader, it is more important to concentrate on the healing results rather than on any other aspect of the Life Memory Recall and Guided Light Therapy process.

Case # 1: Beginning Peak Flow Range 240–260.

Session #1.

Janet is a young woman, married with children. She had suffered from asthma as long as she could remember. We found two past lives whereby she died from lung problems. In one life, she had a very nice life, but died from pneumonia. In the second life she was a young boy who was hated by his father. His father ended the boy's life by holding a pillow over the boy's face and smothering him.

Session #2.

Janet was saddened for a few days by the memory of the young boy who was killed by his father, but she was also feeling more relaxed than before. Her peak flow meter (a device for measuring the amount of air flow when breathing.) went from 475 to 500 without the inhaler and 525 with the use of her inhaler. The normal range for peak flow is 450 to 500.

We found two more past lives that helped to create her asthma in this life. She was a little girl swinging on a swing in her back yard. A dirty, ragged looking man picked her up and took her into the barn. "I am only 4 years old. He pushes himself on me. I don't want him on me." You could hear the fear in her voice as she cried out. "I am surrounded by hay. Hard to breath. He is so heavy. He tried to rape me. He rapes me." The second past life was of a boy who worked on a farm. He was hired help who raked hay. He did it because he needed the money. It made his eyes water and he sneezed a lot. He wore long sleeved shirts because his skin would itch when he was near animals. In this life, Janet also itches when she comes in contact with animals, and she had always had an unexplainable and profound dislike of barns and the smell of hay, avoiding these since childhood if she could.

Session #3.

Janet told me that in general she felt more open and was breathing easier. She was still bothered by the little boy who was smothered and could not breathe. We found several more past lives where she was on a farm or took care of animals. We released them through Guided Light Therapy.

Session #4.

Her peak flow was now continuously around 475–500, and she had reached 525. She used to break out whenever she was near animals, including domestic ones like cats. She related that when she had recently visited a friend who had a cat, she petted it and rubbed her face in his fur, and it did not affect her. In this session, we found a few more past lives that affected her in ways that brought on her many breathing problems, including more of her allergies. One was a young college student, a boy who felt the heavy-handed pressures of his father to do well, which created stress in the young student. He could not please his father. He wanted out. He hanged himself. It was a hard and slow death as the rope suffocated the life out of him. In the second life discovered at this session, Janet was small boy of two who lived on a farm. The farmyard was filled with chickens. The chickens chased after the boy continually. While it was fun at first, he could not get them to stop, and the boy became very frightened. He stayed frightened of chickens for the rest of his life. Janet had experienced allergic reactions when she has been exposed to chickens.

Session #5.

Janet informed me that she tested herself by being in a friend's house with cats and dogs. She petted them and she was ok, no sneezing or watery eyes. Normally her peak flow was in the 300's when she was exposed to animals. But this time it remained at 450 after being with the animals and using her inhaler. During the past week, without the inhaler, her peak flow had continually run between 450–500. Her husband told her that she was smiling more, and that he feels she was feeling better about herself. She had lost four pounds. During this session we discovered several more past lives that were aggravating her asthma. One important one was the life of someone who killed in anger. The person, a male, had been angry throughout the past life and Janet had kept his anger with her. Through Guided Light Therapy she was able to release the anger she found. While in the Light, Janet was asked to come back one more time.

Session #6.

Her weight was still dropping. In general, her asthma was better. On a scale of 1–10, with #10 being at its worst, it was now at about 2. On this session we worked exclusively on accepting all that she had retrieved from the past and releasing it from her current lifetime. Releasing included accepting the fact that she no longer had asthma and she does not have to carry the past with her. By releasing the identified causes of her symptoms, she could release the dis-ease and the expression of the disease. In the Light, Janet released the reasons and causes of her lack of breath, fear and anger—all related one way or another to the suffering she had experienced throughout her life.

Several months later I received this email:

> "Dear Norton,
> Here's an update on my Asthma condition. I don't have any!
> Since our last meeting, my peak flow remains between 500 and 525, without any difference when in the presence of animals. I have since acquired 6 chickens that are now our new pets. I'm happy to say I have had no physical reaction to handling them! I don't sneeze, itch or wheeze when having been around them. In addition, after cleaning out their coop (the smell was pretty strong), I couldn't believe it when I didn't wheeze at all during the process. I know before that would have triggered me without a doubt! I thank the Lord every time I have an experience like that and I don't react. Through your sessions, I believe the Lord has healed me of my Asthma. Thank you for being a

vehicle to let that happen!

I'll keep you posted on any further developments."

Janet's story is not unique. But what makes it unique to us is that her healing has been measured by medical means of evaluation. For many in the traditional medical field, questions about the techniques will arise without the answers they may be looking for. This occurs because the healing possibilities of Life Memory Recall and Guided Light Therapy are only beginning to be understood by modern medicine. For me, as a participant in fostering a wider understanding of the mind and body connection in healing, I will support the medical community by continuing to validate the healing results.

As of this writing, three of the research subjects have reported that their peak flow is within a normal range and two do not need their medications to control an onset of the condition. I have no doubt about the healing outcomes the other research participants will report. The following is what Dr. Silverstein reported:

"Physicians are like any other group of individuals, they promote to others what and how they see the world. The way they see the world is based on habit, experience and tradition. Speaking from my experience, physicians are proud of their tradition, a tradition of scientific exploration. Scientific, as I am referring to it, means that things are studied in what is called the double blind, placebo-controlled, crossover study. This is an absolute gold standard of how scientific studies are done today. However, from what I understand, only about 38% of what physicians do is grounded in such studies. The majority of what they do is instead grounded in experience and what they have been taught. What they have been taught is not based on double blind placebo-controlled crossover studies. Why is this background important?

Because physicians like myself tend to be disbelieving when it comes to alternative medicine. In general, for whatever reasons, as a group this non-acceptance has caused us to turn our backs on these methods of patient care. We have even turned our backs to double blind, placebo-controlled, crossover studies that have been done within the alternative medicine discipline.

Bearing in mind my generalized assessment of physicians' predispositions, education and predigest, I was pleased to have the opportunity to research the effectiveness of Life Memory Recall and Guided Light Therapy with Norton. My evaluation included the patients who had already finished their therapy with Norton and a conference with a pulmonary specialist in my office building. All of Norton's finished case studies' asthma vastly improved, demonstrating normal peak flows at the conclusion of their sessions. I knew that such reports were possible medically, but I still required additional validation. I asked my colleague if such a change in pulmonary function constituted a reality. He said, in fact that it did, that the patients had definitely experienced an improvement in their conditions if their peak flow values changed as it occurred in Norton's preliminary study. Additionally, I have verified that at least one patient is completely free of previous medications. This individual changed nothing else in her life other than working with Norton and the Life Memory Recall process. Returning to my original point, although these findings are not from a double blind, placebo-controlled crossover study, I do believe that these patients' healing results are a valid finding.

Does this make me a convert? No. I must admit, I still find the idea of reincarnation or past lives a bit confusing. I am a "here and now" type of guy and it is hard for me to believe in past lives or recalled life memories. Part of this difficulty stems from my own psychological make-up where the concept of connection while growing up was limited, past life connection being all the more foreign. However, as a physician, I overlooked this personal lack of understanding in the subject matter and concentrated on the potential effectiveness of the therapy. Like Norton, I rely on the results to speak for themselves.

Will I consider including Norton's techniques, Life Memory Recall and Guided Light Therapy, as a part of my treatment plan for asthma control? Yes. I think I can easily recommend it now and in fact, already have. It seems entirely benign, not based on the Western medical model, "what is your problem and what is the correct medicine or surgery?" I believe Norton's approach is a good approach, when it can be applied and when the conventional medical model has little to offer. There are no medications involved in discovering past life memories or invasive procedures of any kind. I strongly recommend this form of treatment, when delivered with the knowledge and care such as Norton provides, for those who are willing to give it a try in search of healing results. As more research is done, in time, we physicians may look upon this work differently, thus expanding our own roles as healers.

H. Robert Silverstein, M.D., F.A.C.C."

With the medical evaluations and healing results now speaking for themselves, I feel confident enough about my work to go out on a limb one last time. What I have left to say about the healing effects of Life Memory Recall and Guided Light Therapy does necessitate my sticking my neck out. At the present time, science cannot back me up. Yet, I know in time it will.

Hollie taught me many things about my own judgments of this work and the limitations that I created myself. It would be impossible to include all the details of how she and the information she retrieved contributed to the development of both techniques: Life Memory Recall and Guided Light Therapy. Hopefully, I have expressed how, through the process of my learning as detailed in this book, there was a subtle yet obvious and knowing guide right beside me. I did not develop the techniques nor pen a single word alone!

After hours of taped sessions with Hollie, we learned not only how to alter my professional ability to help others find healing, but, we also learned a few basic lessons about how each person can begin their healing journey themselves. These lessons, when acknowledged, set the stage for transforming the impossible into possibilities. They are not dependent upon experiencing Life Memory Recall or Guided Light Therapy. This means, for the reader who does not have access to these techniques, at least not yet, there is still something to be gained from reading about them in this book.

There is a place to get started, concepts to think about that may change the reader's perspective and activate healing. Why? Because the concepts that allowed the healing techniques to develop are available for the reader to use, to consider as a beginning step for discovering a path toward healing. And like the past life memory itself, these concepts do not need to be believed to work, they just need to be known, letting the results speak for themselves. Hollie and I hope that by sharing what has been learned, new thoughts that helped us find uncharted avenues of healing, we are sharing a gift that can be applied to anyone's condition or circumstance right now.

First and very simply put: limitations block healing. Limitations come from beliefs that do not allow for the seemingly impossible to exist. These limitations stem from some form of judgment, non-acceptance, emotional hurt, fear or a lack of love. The thoughts and emotions connected to these aspects of ordinary living, deny a person of hope. Without hope that anything can happen, healing opportunities begin to wither. An example is when traditional medicine has done all it can do and yet, dis-ease continues. Since many clients see me as a last resort, I have heard all too often, "I've been told there's nothing more that can be done." If this statement were true, none of the stories in this book could possibly have happened! There is always something that can be done that will contribute to an individual's healing by removing limiting beliefs, one way or another, one form or another.

Second, the heart is always involved in healing. And this is true in a way that may not be easy to state or even comprehend. Hollie talked about it. I listened. We then used the information to develop Guided Light Therapy as a complimentary and added feature of Life Memory Recall. In time, based on the increasing healing results my client's were encountering, I found that what Hollie had said was true. And even though I agree, it is still impossible for me to say why this is so.

She stated in one of our sessions that there is a healing energy connected to the heart, which is neither in it, around it or behind it, but is an inseparable part of it. It is an energy that, when freed, can be used to promote healing. She likened this heart-connected energy to an electron in an atomic cloud.[1] Physicists tell us that electrons exist. What they are really made of no one really knows for sure. Where they exist is anyone's guess. Their exact location cannot truly be pinpointed at any given time because they are always in a state of coming or going. They do not stand still. So, a broader reference is used, one that tells us at least where to look. We say that around the center of an atom, the nucleus, there is a virtual cloud. The electron can be at any point in this cloud at any given time. The cloud exists because it includes the past path of the electron as much as it includes the current and future paths. And depending on a person's perspective, the electron would appear as if it were either coming towards you or away from you. Meaning, that the only difference between perceiving the coming and going, the past, present or future location, is the vantage point of the person who is looking. Time itself then becomes irrelevant and perception is all that matters.

The concept of the cloud can be used to describe the energy that exists around and within the heart and our emotions. If we assume that the heart and its emotions act like the center or nucleus of the atom, we can also assume that the healing heart energy is like the heart's cloud. I have come to call this cloud, "soul stuff". "Soul" because by definition this word means the immaterial essence, animating principle, or actuating cause of an individual life. "Stuff" because the essence is made up of particular things with properties as yet unknown, like the electrons. And like the electron in the cloud, the stuff in the soul cannot be pinpointed and is not time dependent. In other words, the soul stuff is something that does not have limitations of its own. It can be expressed anywhere, anytime. There are no limits to where it can be found other than to know that it is always existing somewhere, at all times, around or within the heart. Just as an electron cloud exists because of its center, the soul stuff exists because of the heart.

The only limitation of soul stuff or healing heart energy is our own perception. Do we see our essence, our actuating cause of life as coming or going? Is our vantage point from the past, present or future? Do we understand that each perspective can offer a different view, a different reality?

---

1. Hollie or "someone" often answered questions in our sessions with complicated and scientifically challenging responses that she and I would have to later decipher. The example portraying the heart connection has been summarized for the reader's convenience.

The key is to not judge anything associated with it. This includes time itself. Since soul stuff is outside of our understanding and measurement, its make-up cannot be pinpointed. When attempts are made to isolate and categorize it, we judge it. This judgment constricts infinite possibilities, making things finite, terminable. In turn, the capabilities of the healing heart energy itself are diminished. It is like viewing an electron as a static round orb. In this form, the electron may be able to be defined but its true nature can never be represented. The inherent power of the whirling electron is lost within such a narrow perspective and so to are its potential and beneficial uses. The same is true of the heart and its whirling energy potential, soul stuff. If viewed narrowly, defined with limited perspective, its potential uses follow suit. And the heart loses its inherent power of healing.

The first time I heard this idea, paraphrased here from Hollie's session, I could not quite grasp what it meant. Yet, it resonated in a way that made sense to me. As Guided Light Therapy developed, based on concepts about the heart, sense turned to fact. More and more clients began using this technique for releasing their discomforts or dis-eases, and they improved. Today, as I have learned even more about the potential of the heart and its healing energy or soul stuff, the more I believe this to be true. So far, the only limitation I have encountered of this energy's healing potential has been the lack of vocabulary to express what it does and how it does it.

Rather than continuing to try to define the concept of heart healing, soul stuff, the irrelevance of time, and the essence of infinite healing possibilities, I have included a story that helps to demonstrate a bit of what I am trying to summarize. Before I provide the details, a few assumptions of understanding are required.

The first assumption, without asking you to adopt my thinking, is that an individual knows many souls or essence of a person from past lives. Again, if we assume that the soul is combined with stuff of life, like a permeating cloud of some kind, then we can assume that essence is forever present regardless of any point in time or location. Meaning that if the essence of a person or soul stuff is not time or location dependent, then it can exist infinitely. The soul stuff of someone yesterday exists no differently than the soul stuff of someone a hundred years ago. Although a very simple and general definition, I have no doubt that it tugs at the core of acceptability for most readers. For this reason, I want to again state that what I am sharing does not have to be believed nor accepted, just not judged. I will attempt to explain further through the use of example.

One broad application of this concept is to use it to explain why we automatically feel comfortable with some strangers. Somehow and for some unknown reason, we meet people and feel as though we have met them before. Our reaction may range from a subtle thought of wondering if you met before to a distinct emotional response, as if there is history shared. Some people may refer to these experiences as Déjà vu. The sessions with my clients have taught me that Déjà vu may be the word used to describe this familiarity feeling, yet there is much more going on than just a feeling.

If time is irrelevant when working in the Light or with soul stuff in regard to healing, then it must be removed from our thinking. Whether a person *actually* knows someone they just met or just *feels* like they actually know the person does not matter. Changing the words is not as important as changing the definition of how a person perceives the event. For Guided Light Therapy, this change in definition means that you can know someone in all ways: physically, psychologically, emotionally or in essence. Knowing someone in essence is the newer, broader sense of definition I am speaking about. Many clients have described this knowing during their sessions. They do not see or hear the person they are conversing with, yet they know who it is and what is being shared. In other words, during the sessions, clients may get the information they need without *actually* conversing with someone else. Vivid images are not always necessary. Additionally, when the information about a lifetime or person in another lifetime is passed to the client via the recalled life memory, it is done so regardless of time: past, present or future. The odds of receiving information from an historic figure is just as great as receiving information from someone who is or was present in a client's current life.

This fact is the very reason that Hollie and I have expanded the techniques of past life regression as I originally learned them and developed Life Memory Recall. We realized quite a while ago that focusing only on lives previously lived was an artificial limit. When I set this limit, I inadvertently limited possibilities for healing for my clients. My work proved to me that I needed to let go of all time constraints in order to achieve the greatest results. Life memories could come from any point in time, including the client's previously lived moments of their current lives. This realization created a greater avenue for healing and the improved results for my clients followed shortly after it was integrated into what I had previously learned. When integrated, Life Memory Recall techniques were made possible.

I became so convinced of the importance of timelessness in my work that this concept has even expanded beyond the definition of past and present. As strange as it may sound, future life memories are possible too! Further discussion of this concept, however, is not included here. Dealing with the limitlessness of the past and present connections is more than enough to keep us thinking.

Therefore, if we accept, at least provisionally, that the soul stuff of people somehow are timeless and location-less, then we can also accept that personal information can be gathered or experienced at any time. And like the electron cloud, the soul essence can be anywhere as well.

This is, in part, a brief description to help you understand why Life Memory Recall and Guided Light Therapy are techniques whereby people can receive the information they need to heal. If soul stuff or healing heart energy carries personal essence everywhere at any time, then all knowledge acquired from any life lived may also be available everywhere at any time. The only challenge would be finding the place to connect at the right time to acquire the knowledge needed. Life Memory Recall and Guided Light Therapy allows an individual the ability to access the soul stuff or essence information they need that contains within it the knowledge to heal.

When dealing with the concept of soul stuff, not only did I need to clear my own judgments but I have also needed to be prepared for anything. The next story illustrates what I mean quite well, using a beyond

Déjà vu example. At a workshop I was giving, I met a young man named Jack. He was in his late twenties. During the session, he talked about his life partner, Bill. When I mentioned something about gay partners, he stood up and said. "I am not gay! Not by the traditional terms anyway. I have never had any gay tendencies throughout my life until I met Bill. I dated women and loved them, and the intimacy between us was very satisfying. Men never appealed to me. I had no desire to meet men on a sexual or intimate level. With Bill it was different. I am sure that I have known him in a past life or many past lives. We were just immediately drawn to each other. A love between us was there, a love I had never felt. If he were a male or female, we would be drawn to each other and be together today."

This gentleman's conviction was absolutely iron clad. He was completely convinced that the knowing between him and his partner was on a much deeper level than the mere physical. Had it not been so, this life change may not have happened. Yet, is it possible that these two men connected on a soul level, one that may have repeated itself in the past? It does not matter. It is more important not to judge the knowing this man feels he has, but to determine whether the results of this possible connection is healing for both men. The exchange did tell me that this man had some understanding that connections occur for people beyond physical reality. He was not the first to say this, nor, I am absolutely sure, will he be the last.

While this connection led to a close relationship between these two men in this lifetime, the reverse of this situation can happen. Just because an individual meets a soul or person essence who they believe they have been with in the past, does not mean that they will or should be with that person in their current life. A person may meet someone and be attracted to him or her instantly, but this person is not necessarily intended to spend this life with the other person. The two individuals may be meeting again to share a healing lesson, feeling or knowledge, then move on to learn another lesson elsewhere.

If we go back to our electron cloud analogy, this situation can be compared to an atom having two electrons in its cloud. There is always a random chance that they will collide. Sometimes the collision is catastrophic and sometimes it brings unity that elevates the atom (aka relationship) to a new and higher level. The possibility of collision is infinite, just as the possible locations of the electrons are in their cloud.

The good news is that, although Guided Light Therapy cannot predict what soul essence may be encountered where or when, it can protect an individual from an unexpected collision leading to catastrophe. It does this by helping a person understand why a previous catastrophe occurred, so as to prevent its repeat in the future or provide the meaning so that the collision will result in unity for a higher level of understanding. From my years of experience, this higher level of understanding is indeed "stuff" of the heart, because love is inevitably involved. Where there is love, fear does not exist. And when fear has been removed, I have witnessed time and time again the beginning of a client's healing results. Love itself is never too far away from any healing effect that occurs. It IS the generating force permeating all healing heart energy.

My clients Jason and Gwen had an experience that exemplifies this. They represent a particularly interesting story of a love lost, a love found and a healing through meaning.

As the couple told me, "They were at a large conference sitting across from each other at a table having lunch. There were a number of individuals at the table trying to make small talk. They were people of common interest, yet were individuals who had never met before they joined each other for lunch. The conversation was simple, the kind one often finds when people are trying to make polite and hopefully interesting conversation with people they do not know. As the conversation continued, two faces across the table noticed each other. Their attention was constantly drawn toward each other. As the day went on their paths crossed several times. Each time they met, they felt an increasing attraction growing between them. As they described it, it was more of a feeling of comfort or familiarity.

When the conference was winding down, several small groups gathered discussing the conference issues and related subjects. These two strangers found themselves in one of these small, conversational groups. They were together, talking, being a part of the group, yet not truly a part of the group, and both silently aware that being with the group was an excuse to be in each other's presence.

It approached dinnertime, and the groups started to break up for the day. As the crowd was dispersing, out of character, Jason asked Gwen if she wanted to join him for dinner. Because she had some pressing things to attend to that evening, she hesitantly declined. They said their good-byes and went to give each other a friendly hug, having enjoyed the little bits of exchange throughout the day. They both felt that it had been a truly interesting and pleasant day, and both knew that they would probably never see each other again. The hug turned out to be something very unexpected and shocking. To their surprise, as they hugged each other, a warm gripping shock went through each of them. It was not an electrical shock, sharp and stinging, but a pleasant, gentle continuous jolt going through both of their bodies. They looked at each, bemused and surprised. They separated to arms length and stared at each other for a moment. Both were befuddled, flustered, confused, and did not know what to make of it. Having not uttered a word during these fleeting moments, both were thinking to themselves silently, "It must be my imagination." Spontaneously, as if to test what had happened and their imaginations, they reached toward each other and hugged again. It had the same startling results. Again, they both felt the strangely new yet pleasant shock going right through them as they embraced.

They did go to dinner that night. As they tell it, they were instantly comfortable with each other, drawn to each other with complete openness. It was as though they had known each other forever. Actually, it turns out that they had.

Several weeks after the conference, this couple set up an appointment to see me. I say couple, because their continued familiarity with each other made me feel as if I were speaking to a long married couple. I understood that they had barely met, yet, in some respects, to call them a couple felt more right than not. They said they did not mind if I continued to refer to them that way.

They had conversed a few times since the conference and had identified several issues they wished to explore. The primary issue was, "Did they have any past lives together?" So, we began there. Although they came as a couple, during the sessions, I worked with each individually. The past life memories revealed were shared later.

We discovered that they had been together many times in past lives. Each memory we encountered repeatedly demonstrated a wonderful, warm and close relationship. They were husband and wife or lovers in more than thirty past lives. They were so intertwined in their past that when one would die and go to the Light, the other would be there waiting to welcome them. Regardless of which individual I was working with, responses during the Guided Light Therapy portion of the session were exactly the same. There were no deviations. The same continuous pattern emerged regardless of whom I was having a session with. In the Light, they would be with each other again and again, always. More importantly to them, they met in the Light after each past life had reached its end, with the love they still held for each other. Their love had grown stronger with each added past life memory we found. Here is an example of one of their lives together.

They were in the tall grass rolling around together, making love. It was in England in the 1600's and they were young lovers, 15 and 16 years old. It was their first love and in that life would be their only true love. They both came from affluent families. Where they frolicked in the tall grass, their two large family estates could be seen in the distant, sweeping hills. Fortunately, this place was a place where they could not be seen. They had to hide their feelings for each other, as their families had already picked their future marriage partners. They were not chosen for each other.

The love between them was intense and complete, a true first love, the kind of love that is remembered always. They ate, drank and breathed each other as if they were one; male and female, separate yet joined. They fit perfectly. Sadly, they never married each other. They followed their families' wishes and married the spouse chosen for them. She died at age 37 from a heart problem. He died shortly thereafter. She greeted him when he came up to the Light.

Again they were together like they had been so many other times. They discovered and explored various and numerable past life memories. The result was always the same. At the end of each life, when the last of the two had passed on, the other was waiting in the Light, always in love with each other, always happy, always bound together as one.

At this point you may expect that the two people who came to see me became one and lived together happily ever after in this life. After all, who would not think that after experiencing so much love through the Life Memory Recall and Guided Light Therapy process that these two people would want to be apart, especially after what they had experienced in our sessions.

But that was not the way it was meant to be. The information and meaning that came from the past life memories of these two people helped them understand their uncanny and strange immediate reaction to each other. They understood that they had their own separate lives to live. Our work together allowed them to explore unseen connections. From these connections, they could improve upon their own lives and the lives of each other in ways that were beneficial, not destructive. They realized they met and are here to learn from each other. They are here to cherish each other and help each other, not necessarily be with each other. There is work to be done together. They are to teach and enlighten others. They are to spread the love between them in a way that helps others, in a way that benefits people in their own lives. This is part of their growth, understanding and self-love for their current lifetime. By encountering each other, they enhanced their individual purpose for being. It has since emotionally healed them both.

Not all wonderful past life memories where couples were together means that the same two people are to be together now. If by chance you meet someone with whom you have this type of connection, or they with you, it does not mean that the present life situation must be drastically changed. It does not mean that the two of you are to leave your families and go off to lead an idyllic life together. Generally, we are with our family to learn lessons. Leaving does not necessarily mean greater lessons or advancement in a person's healing journey. By leaving, we often miss the special opportunity we have to learn and grow from the experiences and choices we have already made.

When someone comes into our lives it might be to serve as a simple reminder of happier times or it could be a lesson from a past life to be re-experienced as a way to open our awareness. There are infinite possibilities of meaning for this and other kinds of recognition. The idea of soul stuff or personal essence being one of the most common possibilities I have heard, although not necessarily using the words Hollie and I have come to know. Regardless of the mechanism for these feelings, the feelings need to be addressed, and Life Memory Recall and Guided Light Therapy are safe and healing ways to accomplish this.

Feelings generated by a sense of knowing can be overpowering. They are especially gripping when they involve love. Through my work, the emotional reactions that could cause someone to move in a direction disruptive in their lives can be redirected by gaining an understanding of the experience of connection. I have met several people whom I personally have had this connection with in a past life. I take them into the Light to find out why we are together again. It is always positive, a means to help each other, to learn from each other. Often the lessons to be learned are very simple lessons. Frequently the lessons are as simple as to love one another, appreciate nature, learn to be kind to people who you might not have been kind to before, et cetera. These kinds of simple lessons have had such a great healing value for my clients. They have had the same effect on me.

I now view things very differently. I no longer see things in black and white. I see so many shades of gray along with other beautiful colors that mingle and intertwine. There is a kind of brightness in the colors of life that I have never seen before. My myopic view of the world has changed and widened. My acceptance of situations and people has grown. In the past, I most likely would have ignored much of what I now find wonderful in its variety and difference. Less judgment has opened my heart in ways that has added close and loving friends. I now believe that we are all one, that all soul stuff is somehow wonderfully connected. With a belief in the timelessness of personal essence, this is no longer an imaginary stretch.

I can no longer treat anyone poorly because I can no longer treat anyone differently than I would treat myself. This has increased my capacity to openly love. The lesson of non-judgment has broken and dissipated fears that previously existed. Barriers and limitations to the realm of infinite possibilities have been removed.

My heart has been continually mending, the healing energy pouring out more freely. As a result, various physical ailments and personal discomforts have been relieved. I have firmly come to believe that nothing is ever without hope of positive healing change.

I now know we are all healers. We can heal ourselves. We can heal each other. The kind word, the smile and the sense of love coming through us touches others, and when it does, it heals. It is my belief that we heal ourselves by accepting love, we heal others by giving love. In this way, the heart and everything around it, in it and of it becomes the most effective and powerful healing tool yet.

Life was and is full of lessons. All I had to do was simply learn them and accept them, taking them into my heart to find the real value. I realized that the hard times, the difficulties I have gone through are learning experiences. It may not be easy to believe at first, but I now see these difficult times as gifts, gifts teaching priceless lessons. The sharing of the difficulties of my clients only brought me closer to seeing and understanding the value each lesson provides.

I know that Life Memory Recall and Guided Light Therapy are ways to discover and uncover the meaning that allows this kind of learning to take place in a comfortable way. I know that by releasing any lessons and understandings that are based in fear or guilt or sadness or any other less than loving feelings, the door to the realm of possibilities is found. And by going through it, an individual taps into his or her own energy source that provides them the capacity to heal. I have learned the lesson that I cannot possibly determine what dis-eases or illnesses can or cannot be healed. Anything is possible and many of the stories I have shared indicate that this is true.

As Hollie said at our first meeting, "Healing, it's in the heart: the heart is where the healing occurs." That means that with an adjustment in the physical, psychological, emotional or spiritual parts of us with love and the wisdom of the Light, any of these things can be changed. There is no healing that does not have hope when change is made possible. And when the heart has hope its healing energy is released.

Working together, Hollie and I have come to believe in what "someone" said in our early sessions, "The heart is a place where answers can be found." It took us both a while afterward to understand and accept the lessons that Life Memory Recall and Guided Light Therapy have taught us and how these lessons provided the meaning behind "someone's" words. It took us even longer to see the path that would eventually guide us where we needed to go.

Hollie and I wish you all a wonderful journey of healing and a life to be enjoyed.

For More Information

Visit the **Healing Power Of Our Past** Website:

www.thehealingpowerofourpast.com

Or In Writing:

P. O. Box 116
Storrs, CT. 06268

About the Authors

Norton Berkowitz, Ph.D., has been advancing the knowledge of human healing as a hypnotherapist and facilitator of Past Life Regression therapy for more than 20 years. As Director of the Life Memory Recall Research Foundation, Norton has brought new understanding and improved therapeutic techniques to people, traditional practitioners and researchers worldwide.

Hollie Martin, D.D.S., Ph.D. has more than 15 years of experience in practicing traditional and alternative healing methods and has worked extensively as a facilitator in improving human potential. Hollie is currently working as a human resource specialist in transforming organizational cultures for a Fortune 100 company.

978-0-595-34924-1
0-595-34924-2

Printed in the United States
34226LVS00004B/76-96

9 780595 349241